D1345774

A gift given with love to:

....

Andrew   Patrick   Hawthorne

....

From:

Nana & Papa......

on the occasion of his

.............baptism.............

7.8.2016

My 1st
Books and More

Carine Mackenzie and
Philip Ross

CF4·K

10 9 8 7 6 5 4 3 2 1
Copyright © Carine Mackenzie 2016
Let's Think About Bible Prayers © Philip Ross 2016
ISBN: 978-1-78191-748-0

Published in 2016 by
Christian Focus Publications Ltd.
Geanies House, Fearn, Ross-shire,
IV20 1TW, Scotland, U.K.
www.christianfocus.com

Cover design by Daniel van Straaten
Printed and bound in China

Contents

THEOLOGY AND FAMILIES

Let's Think About Theology... that is what this book is here to help you do, to think about God and who he is and what he does. To think about who you are in relation to God and how you can have a relationship with him.

Quite a few years ago I started a series of books called My 1st... one book led to another until there were ten little volumes in the set, including one written by Philip Ross (*My 1st Book of Bible Prayers*). The teaching in these books was aimed at children but I've discovered over the years that the same material has also been of benefit to adults.

The simple question and answer format in *My 1st Book of Questions and Answers* has been a method of teaching doctrine for centuries, and with updated language, families have rediscovered this tool of learning from the past. It's great to hear of families and churches who are using this little book with the next generation.

The other books have key Scriptures and brief lessons — ideal for family devotional times. Using one of these readings every day will make your home into a valuable theological seminary for your children.

Collecting all these titles together in one volume is a practical way of having all this teaching and Scripture available to you in one place. However, there is some new material too — Look out for the new section on the Psalms.

So this book now totals 371 different readings. One for every day of the year and more! Each reading has at least one Scripture verse to accompany it and a brief lesson. After every seventh reading or so you will find a section called Question, Answer and Memory. Each of these has a couple of questions and answers, as well as a memory verse to memorize. The questions and answers come from: My 1st Book of Questions and Answers and the verses come from: My 1st Book of Memory Verses.

There is also an index at the back of the book that covers key topics. So if you want to focus on a particular characteristic of God or an aspect of his Word you can use this tool to give that focus to your devotions.

I hope that you find this book to be of encouragement to you and your family, that you will learn about God and his Word through these pages.

Please have His Word open beside you as you read through this book, as nothing replaces the actual Word of God. When you have time read the memory verses and other scriptures in their context. Encourage your children and yourself to read, learn and memorize the Word of God together.

Carine Mackenzie

KEY POINTS
1. 366 Readings
2. 114 Questions and Answers
3. 53 different Memory Verses
4. Ideal for family devotions
5. Scripture and Topical Index

NOTE FROM THE AUTHOR

In writing the Questions and Answers throughout this book I found the Shorter Catechism and Willison's Mother's Catechism of immense help in deciding on a structure and what to include.

Let's Think About
CHRISTIAN
VALUES

1. Christian Values

Love the LORD your God and keep his requirements, his decrees, his laws and his commands always. (Deuteronomy 11:1 NIV)

God has given us instructions in his Word about how we should live and what we should say and what we should think. We are sinful when we are born and we do, say and think things that are wrong every day. But the Lord Jesus Christ, the Son of God came to this earth to save us from our sins.

Through his death we have forgiveness for sins. He lived the perfect life that we find impossible. Yet by his grace our lives can be changed and with his help we can try to live in a way that is pleasing to God. When we fail, the Lord is willing to forgive, if we come to him and ask for forgiveness.

2. Admit You are Wrong

Confess your sins to one another and pray for one another. (James 5:16)

When we do something wrong, we sometimes try to cover it up or to make excuses and blame someone else. The right thing to do is to admit that we are wrong and to say sorry. It is most important that we admit our sins to God and say sorry to him.

Jesus told a story about a son who left home and behaved badly. When he came to his senses and his need was great, he decided to go back home and tell his father he had sinned. The father welcomed him with open arms. This story shows how God welcomes sinners to himself.

3. Appreciation of Others

Outdo one another in showing honour. (Romans 12:10)

How often we say 'Me first!' We want the first turn, the best seat or the biggest piece of cake. God tells us to think and act differently. You ought to think of: Jesus – first, Others – next, Yourself – last

If you have Jesus, Others, Yourself in that order – that spells JOY.

4. Care about Speech

Let no corrupting talk come out of your mouths, but only such as is good for building up, as fits the occasion, that it may give grace to those who hear. (Ephesians 4:29)

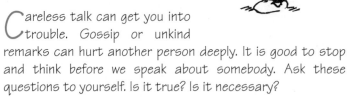

Careless talk can get you into trouble. Gossip or unkind remarks can hurt another person deeply. It is good to stop and think before we speak about somebody. Ask these questions to yourself. Is it true? Is it necessary?

God hears every word. Make sure that what you say is true, kind, pure and wholesome. Jesus warned us that we will have to give an account of every idle word, in the day of judgement (Matthew 12:36).

Our words indicate the state of our heart. Evil words come from an evil heart. Good words should come from a heart changed by the Lord Jesus Christ.

5. Confidence in God

Trust in the L ORD with all your heart, and do not lean on your own understanding. In all your ways acknowledge him, and he will make straight your paths. (Proverbs 3:5, 6)

God is in control and does everything well. Even when life is tough and things seem to be going wrong, God understands. When we trust in our own abilities we will make big mistakes.

Peter the disciple boasted that he would never deny the Lord Jesus, but he failed miserably. He was trusting in himself at that point rather than in God.

God has promised guidance and direction when we commit everything to him. Jesus encouraged his followers to believe God and trust in him. 'Let not your hearts be troubled. Believe in God; believe also in me,' he said (John 14:1).

6. Contentment

Godliness with contentment is great gain. (1 Timothy 6:6)
Be content with what you have. (Hebrews 13:5)

Sometimes we can be so unhappy because we wish we were better looking, or more clever or had more money. God tells us that it is a great blessing to be content with what we have. Happiness does not depend on things or circumstances. True happiness is from God.

Paul, who had many hardships in his life, could say that he had learned to be content in any situation (Philippians 4:11). We should pray that we would learn to be content too.

7. Forgiveness

Be kind to one another, tenderhearted, forgiving one another, as God in Christ forgave you. (Ephesians 4:32)

If someone does something hurtful or makes an unkind remark about you, how do you react? Do you want to get your own back? Perhaps say or do something unkind too?

God tells us to be forgiving, remembering that we also do and say what is wrong. We need forgiveness from God through Jesus Christ and so we ought to give forgiveness to others through Jesus Christ.

Ask God to help you to show forgiveness. Jesus himself prayed for those who were nailing him to the cross. 'Father, forgive them, for they do not know what they are doing' (Luke 23:34 NIV).

QUESTION, ANSWER AND MEMORY

1. Who made you?
God. (Genesis 1:27)
2. Why did God make you?
To glorify him and enjoy him. (1 Corinthians 10:31)
3. What else did God make?
God made all things. (Genesis 1:31)

MEMORY VERSE 1
In the beginning God created the heavens and the earth (Genesis 1:1)
Everything in this universe was made by God. He had no beginning and will have no end – He is eternal. He is worthy of our praise and honour.

8. Generosity

Each one must give as he has decided in his heart, not reluctantly or under compulsion, for God loves a cheerful giver. (2 Corinthians 9:7)

It is good to have a friend who is willing to share with us. If we are mean and selfish, we will be very unhappy.

God tells us to give what we can to others and to him – share our possessions and give our time to those in need, simply and cheerfully.

Jesus tells us to give to others without any fuss – not telling everybody what we have given (Matthew 6:3).

This shows true love. Jesus showed the greatest love by giving us the greatest gift – himself.

9. Gentleness

The fruit of the Spirit is 'gentleness' ... (Galatians 5:23)
A servant of the Lord must not quarrel but be gentle to all. (2 Timothy 2:24 NKJV)

When God the Holy Spirit works in our heart, he gives gentleness. This makes us careful and considerate of others who are weak or fragile. We will not treat them roughly.

To be gentle is not a sign of weakness. Jesus, the perfect man, was gentle in dealing with sinners. He is described as a shepherd who gathers the lambs and gently leads the sheep. To be like Jesus is to be gentle.

10. Goodness

The fruit of the Spirit is 'goodness, …. (Galatians 5:22)
Let us not grow weary of doing good … As we have opportunity, let us do good to everyone. (Galatians 6:9, 10)

God, our Creator, commands us to obey him and his Word. To do otherwise is sin. We are born as sinners and do, say and think what is sinful.

God, through Jesus Christ, deals with our sinful natures and actions.

Only with his help can we do what is good. Jesus tells us to do good to others – feed, clothe, visit – and in doing good to others we are doing it for him.

11. Hard Work

Whatever you do, work heartily, as for the Lord and not for men. (Colossians 3:23)

Do you only work well in class when the teacher is watching you? Do you have to be told several times to do a task before you set to it? That is not pleasing to God. He wants us to work diligently and do our best for him.

The little ant is commended in the book of Proverbs for being busy and working hard. We would be wise to be like that (Proverbs 6:6).

The work that needs our attention most of all is prayer and studying God's Word.

12. Helpfulness

Bear one another's burdens, and so fulfil the law of Christ. (Galatians 6:2)

Our help is from God. He is a very present help in trouble. He can use people like us to give the needed help.

Jesus told a story about a traveller who was attacked by robbers on the road. The first two men who came by (a priest and a Levite) did not help at all. Then a Samaritan man came along. He helped the injured man, dressed his wounds and took him to an inn to recover – paying for his board and lodgings. Jesus commended this behaviour to us. The Samaritan was a true helpful friend.

13. Honesty

Whatever is true or honest ... think on these things. (Philippians 4:8)

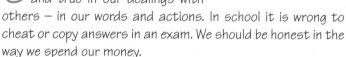

God requires us to be honest and true in our dealings with others – in our words and actions. In school it is wrong to cheat or copy answers in an exam. We should be honest in the way we spend our money.

When we work for an employer we should be honest about the way we spend our time – not using the boss's time for doing our own business. Other people may not discover a dishonest action, but God always knows – even our dishonest thoughts. Ask him to help you to make the right choices and to be honest.

14. Honouring your Parents

Honour your father and your mother. (Exodus 20:12)
Children, obey your parents in the Lord, for this is right. (Ephesians 6:1)

One of God's Ten Commandments is to honour your father and your mother. This means showing them respect and obeying them.

The Lord Jesus showed respect to Mary and Joseph and was obedient to them. Even when he was dying, he had great concern for his mother, asking his friend John to take care of her.

It displeases God when we are cheeky to our parents or disobey them or complain about what they ask us to do. God tells us to listen to the instruction of our father and to keep the law of our mother (Proverbs 1:8).

QUESTION, ANSWER AND MEMORY

4. Why did God make all things?
For his own glory. (Revelation 4:11)
5. Where does God teach us to praise and enjoy him?
In his Word, the Bible. (John 5:39)
6. Who wrote the Bible?
Holy men who were taught by the Holy Spirit. (2 Timothy 3:16)

MEMORY VERSE 2
Trust ye in the Lord forever; for in the LORD JEHOVAH is everlasting strength (Isaiah 26:4 KJV). God has power and great strength. Because God is so strong, we can safely trust in him.

15. Humility

God opposes the proud, but gives grace to the humble. (James 4:6)

How easy it is to be proud of what we do. We often think too highly of ourselves. We should learn from Jesus Christ who was lowly in heart. He took the place of the servant, washing the disciples' feet.

One day Jesus called over a little child. 'Whoever humbles himself like this little child' he said, 'will be the greatest in the kingdom of heaven' (Matthew 18:4).

Jesus is the greatest example of humility. As the Son of God, he humbled himself and came to our wicked world as a baby, and died on the cross to save his people from their sins.

16. Joy

The fruit of the Spirit is ... joy .... (Galatians 5:22)
Restore to me the joy of your salvation. (Psalm 51:12)

True joy or happiness comes from God. Even when times are hard, or we are sick or lonely, we can experience joy in our hearts when we remember that God is in control and he does everything well.

One great reason to have joy is the fact that our sins are forgiven, when we trust in Christ Jesus and what he has done for us.

Heaven will be a place of perfect joy. 'You have made known to me the path of life; you will fill me with joy in your presence, with eternal pleasures at your right hand' (Psalm 16:11 NIV).

17. Kindness

Love is patient and kind.
(1 Corinthians 13:4)

One evidence of God's love in our hearts is kindness. Joseph was treated very badly by his brothers but years later he became a very important man in Egypt. Because he was so powerful he could easily have punished his brothers, but instead he was kind to them.

'I will look after you and your little ones,' he told them. He spoke kindly to them (Genesis 50:21).

Kindness is more than just giving someone a gift. It involves an attitude of love and willingness to forgive, like Joseph. The Lord has forgiven us so much, so we should forgive others.

QUESTION, ANSWER AND MEMORY

7. What is God?
God is a spirit. (John 4:24)
8. What is a spirit?
An invisible being who does not have a body like us.
(Colossians 1:15)
9. Where is God?
God is everywhere. (Job 11:7)

MEMORY VERSE 3
The eternal God is your refuge, and underneath are the everlasting arms (Deuteronomy 33:27 NIV). A refuge is a safe place to be. When a father wants to keep his little child safe, he puts his arms around him and underneath him. God is the best loving Father.

18. Love

The fruit of the Spirit is love … (Galatians 5:22)
Let us love one another, for love is from God. (1 John 4:7)

You will have heard this phrase before: 'Actions speak louder than words.' It is a very true saying. Showing real Christian love is more than just saying 'I love you'. It requires giving willing and costly service to another person — putting ourselves out in doing something for them.

Jesus tells us that we even have to love our enemies. If we are able to pray for them and wish them well, then we are showing them the love of Christ.

Our first duty is to love God with all our heart, soul, strength and mind. We love him because he first loved us. Our second duty is to love our neighbour as ourselves.

19. Loyalty

A faithful man will abound with blessings. (Proverbs 28:20)

A true friend is loyal and constant. Our first loyalty is to God. He wishes us to be loyal and true to our family and friends.

Ruth showed great loyalty to her widowed mother-in-law, Naomi. 'Don't ask me to leave you,' she said. 'Where you go, I will go; where you stay I will stay. Your people will be my people; and your God, my God' (Ruth 1:16).

A true friend will help in times of trouble and support even when others are critical and nasty.

20. Meekness

Blessed are the meek, for they shall inherit the earth. (Matthew 5:5)

When you have a problem do you lash out and make a fuss? Or are you meek, showing restraint and patient self-control? Meekness is not weakness. It requires strength of character and help from God.

Jesus told us to learn from him and to follow him — for he is meek and lowly in heart. He is the best example for us. He has lived the perfect life for us.

21. Obedience

You shall walk after the LORD your God and fear him, and keep his commandments and obey his voice. (Deuteronomy 13:4)

God requires us to obey his Word. He has given us the Bible to guide us. King Saul did not obey God's commands, instead he kept some animals to sacrifice to God. But God was not pleased with him. 'To obey is better than sacrifice,' Saul was told (1 Samuel 15:22).

Jesus told the story of the two men who each built a house. The wise man built his house on the rock. His house was strong enough to stand during the rain and storm. The man who hears God's words and does them is like that wise man.

We should pray for understanding and willingness to obey God's law.

22. Patience

The fruit of the Spirit is ... patience ....
(Galatians 5:22)
Be still before the LORD and wait patiently for
him. (Psalm 37:7)

If you are playing with your friends it is good
to wait for your turn without becoming upset. If Mum or Dad
has promised to take you swimming later on, you should not keep
pestering them and asking again and again if it is time to go yet.

We must also wait patiently for God's answer to prayer.
Sometimes he says 'No'; sometimes 'Yes' and at other times
he says, 'Just wait for a bit, my time is best.'

Job waited patiently for God to deliver him from his hard
situation. He lost his family, his property and his health. But
he did not complain. He trusted patiently in God. (Job 1:21)

23. Peace

The fruit of the Spirit is ... peace .... (Galatians 5:22)
The peace of God, which surpasses all understanding, will guard
your hearts and your minds in Christ Jesus. (Philippians 4:7)

Sometimes life can be difficult. We might get into trouble
with a teacher or fall out with a friend. It feels like being in
a storm. We can be afraid, sick, lonely or sad. But if we trust
in Jesus he gives us inner peace in the middle of our stormy
life. He gives us the confidence to know that God reigns and
that he is able and willing to do what is best for his children.

Joseph had many problems when he was taken to Egypt.
He suffered slavery, being falsely accused and sent to prison.
But God was with him. God meant it all for good.

24. Purity

So flee youthful passions and pursue righteousness, faith, love, and peace, along with those who call on the Lord from a pure heart. (2 Timothy 2:22)

Be careful about what goes into your mind. God tells us to fix our thoughts on what is true, honourable, right, pure, lovely and admirable (Philippians 4:8). If our minds are taken up with impure thoughts, our actions will soon follow.

Joseph was a slave in Egypt in Potiphar's house, but the Lord was with him. Potiphar's wife was a scheming woman who tried to trick Joseph into impure behaviour. Joseph fled from the room to escape. 'How can I do this great wickedness and sin against God?' he asked. God was important in his life and uppermost in his thoughts and he was helped to flee from youthful passions.

QUESTION, ANSWER AND MEMORY

10. Did God have a beginning?
No. He has always existed. (Psalm 90:2)
11. Will he have an end?
No. He will always exist. (Psalm 102:27)

MEMORY VERSE 4
The Lord bless you and keep you (Numbers 6:24). This prayer is that God would be kind and good to us and preserve us from all harm.

25. Respect for Authority

Let every person be subject to the governing authorities. For there is no authority except from God, and those that exist have been instituted by God. (Romans 13:1)

God has placed us in ordered societies which is a great benefit to us. The rules of the land are made for our good and safety, and to help us to live peaceably with other people. It is our duty to pray for those in authority that they would be given wisdom to rule well.

David showed respect for Saul because he was the king. Saul was an enemy of David, but when David had the chance to retaliate, he showed respect for Saul and did not harm him.

26. Respect for Life

God created man in his own image, in the image of God he created him; male and female he created them. (Genesis 1:27)
I praise you, for I am fearfully and wonderfully made. (Psalm 139:14)

Human life is valuable, a special part of God's creation not just another animal. We must do all we can to protect life and to respect it.

God has given gifts and talents to doctors and surgeons and others in the medical professions, to care for life and to heal many diseases.

God alone decides the time of our death. 'It is appointed for man to die once' (Hebrews 9:27). Death and life are in God's control.

27. Right Choices

Choose this day whom you will serve, … but as for me and my house, we will serve the Lord. (Joshua 24:15)

We make choices every day. If we make a wrong choice, that can lead to problems. Choosing bad company or taking a foolish risk can lead to danger.

Making right choices day by day will help us to make right choices at the important crossroads in our lives. Ask God to help you in your little decisions and in the big ones.

28. Self-control

The fruit of the Spirit is … self-control …. (Galatians 5:23)
Let every person be quick to hear, slow to speak, slow to anger. (James 1:19)

How easy it is to give in to our bad temper or sinful passions and let them control our behaviour and words. To exercise self-control we must be under God's control. Ask him to control your life so that your actions, thoughts and feelings are pleasing to him and not out of control. Sometimes it is right to be angry.

Jesus was angry with those who were abusing God's house by using it for commerce. He overthrew their tables because he was angry. This was not a fit of temper. He was in complete control.

29. Sympathy

Have … sympathy, brotherly love, a tender heart, and a humble mind. (1 Peter 3:8)
Weep with those who weep. (Romans 12:15)

Many people in our world have great suffering – hunger, sickness, disability, loneliness. We should try to remember these people, pray for them and help where possible.

God tells us to be sympathetic to those in prison who need our help and love. There are some people in prison because of their love for the Lord Jesus. God tells us to remember them as if we are in prison with them.

Perhaps all we can do is listen to a friend who shares a problem with us, or give a word of encouragement.

30. Thankfulness

Give thanks in all circumstances. (1 Thessalonians 5:18)
Giving thanks always and for everything to God the Father in the name of our Lord Jesus Christ. (Ephesians 5:20)

If someone offers you a gift, how rude it would be to take it without saying thank you. God our loving Father has given us many marvellous gifts – family, home, friends. Remember to thank him. Jesus once healed ten men who had a terrible skin disease. Only one of these men came back to say thank you and Jesus noticed that. The most wonderful gift that God has given us is the Saviour, the Lord Jesus Christ. Thank God for Jesus, the best gift ever.

31. Truthfulness

Whoever speaks the truth gives honest evidence, but a false witness utters deceit.
(Proverbs 12:17)

God warns us about the dangers of telling lies. The words we speak should be true. We are guided to know what is true by the Bible, God's Word. It is the truth.

Jesus told us that he was 'the truth'. If we trust in him and follow his Word we will be helped to know the truth and to tell the truth.

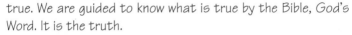

QUESTION, ANSWER AND MEMORY

12. Does God ever change?
No. He is always the same. (Psalm 102:27)
13. Does God know everything?
Yes. Nothing can be hidden from him. (Psalm 44:21)
14. Can God do everything?
Yes. He can do everything that pleases him. (Isaiah 40:13)

MEMORY VERSE 5
The Lord is good to those who wait for him, to the soul who seeks him (Lamentations 3:25). God does not always answer our prayers immediately. It is good for us to wait patiently for him and to realise that he does everything well and at the best time.

32. Wisdom

The fear of the Lord is the beginning of wisdom. (Proverbs 9:10)

Wisdom is not just knowing a lot of facts and being clever. The wise person puts God first in his life. Wisdom is learned from God and his Word.

Young Timothy was taught the Bible by his mother and grandmother from his early years. This made him truly wise, leading to his salvation through Jesus Christ.

NOTE FROM THE AUTHOR

Children want to know what to do. They want to know why we do the things we do. They are full of questions and they need answers.

As well as amazing minds, their souls need direction and care. The foundations that are laid in their young lives will stand firm into adult life. Together with the ministry of the Holy Spirit, Christian principles will be eternal, life-changing values.

In a world where basic moral standards are ignored children need to be taught the truths of humility, generosity, purity and respect. You don't need to teach children to do wrong but you do need to teach them to do right – and to trust in the only one who is good – God.

Let's Think About

THE GOSPEL

33. The Gospel

For by grace you have been saved through faith. And this is not your own doing; it is the gift of God. (Ephesians 2:8)

The gospel is more than the story of Jesus that we read in Matthew, Mark, Luke and John. The good news – or gospel – is God's message to us about his Son, Jesus Christ, who died for sinners. Through repentance and faith in him, sinners can be made right with God.

There are many definitions of the gospel in the Bible. The Bible is full of good news of God's salvation. By God's grace we believe the gospel and trust in Jesus Christ.

May God bring you to thank him for his gospel and to pass the good news on to someone else.

34. The Gospel is Good News

The beginning of the gospel of Jesus Christ, the Son of God. (Mark 1:1)

Gospel means 'good news' – the good news about God's Son, Jesus Christ.

The good news is that Jesus Christ died for sinners. Those who repent and trust in him have their sins forgiven and are made right with God. They receive the gift of eternal life.

Matthew, Mark, Luke and John wrote books which tell this message of Jesus or gospel.

The word gospel appears many times in the Bible. We should thank God for this good news.

35. The Gospel Foretold

Paul ... set apart for the gospel of God, which he promised beforehand through his prophets in the holy Scriptures. (Romans 1:1-2)

The gospel, or good news about the Saviour, was promised for a long time before Jesus was born. Jesus' defeat of the devil was hinted at in the Garden of Eden (Genesis 3:15). Isaiah prophesied hundreds of years before it happened, that a child would be born who would be very special(Isaiah 9:6). His name would be Wonderful Counsellor, Mighty God, Everlasting Father, Prince of Peace. Micah foretold that the child would be born in Bethlehem. Many details of Jesus' life and death were prophesied in the Old Testament, and were fulfilled exactly. (Micah 5:2)

God kept all his promises in Jesus Christ the Saviour.

36. The Saviour is Here

The angel said to them, 'Fear not, for behold, I bring you good news of great joy that will be for all the people. For unto you is born this day in the city of David a Saviour, who is Christ the Lord.' (Luke 2:10-11)

An angel brought good news to the shepherds, telling them of the birth of the Saviour. This was good news, not only for them, but for all people – good news for us today.

God the Son came to this world as a human baby, lived the perfect life here and died to pay the price for our sins.

God's plan of salvation for his people brings us great joy.

37. The Light of the Gospel

The god of this world has blinded the minds of the unbelievers, to keep them from seeing the light of the gospel of the glory of Christ, who is the image of God. (2 Corinthians 4:4)

Jesus is our guiding light in this dark world. He said he is the light of the world. The gospel is like a light too – guiding our path, giving us warmth and safety and help on our journey through life.

Darkness is very scary and dangerous. What good news that Jesus rescues us from that and gives us light.

38. The Gospel of Peace

As shoes for your feet ... put on the readiness given by the gospel of peace. (Ephesians 6:15)

Jesus has promised to give us lasting peace in our heart. Our sin gives us a troubled conscience, a feeling of unease, guilt and anxiety, knowing we are not right with God. We have peace with God through our Lord Jesus Christ when we trust in him.

39. The Gospel of Truth

Of this (hope) you have heard before in the word of truth, the gospel, which has come to you, as indeed in the whole world it is bearing fruit and increasing. (Colossians 1:5-6)

The words of the gospel of Jesus are true. Jesus himself is the truth that leads us to God. False teachers will lead us astray to disaster. But the truth of the gospel will lead us safely on the journey of life to our final destination in heaven with the Lord Jesus.

QUESTION, ANSWER AND MEMORY

15. Can you see God?
No. I cannot see God but he always sees me. (Colossians 1:15)
16. How many gods are there?
There is only one God. (Isaiah 45:5; Deuteronomy 6:4)

MEMORY VERSE 6
We love him (God), because he first loved us (1 John 4:19). We know we love someone when we long to speak with them, we long to hear from them, we want to spend time with them. We love God when we honour him, obey him, want to do what pleases him. We can only do that because he has first loved us.

40. The Gospel of the Kingdom

And this gospel of the kingdom will be proclaimed throughout the whole world as a testimony to all nations. (Matthew 24:14)

A king is a ruler of a kingdom. There is a great kingdom made up of all God's people. Its ruler is Jesus Christ.

Jesus told several parables (or stories) to describe his kingdom. Although it may seem small and insignificant, it has a great effect and is very precious. The good news (gospel) of the kingdom will reach through the whole world. His kingdom can be found wherever there are people who trust and obey Jesus.

41. The Gospel of your Salvation

In him (Christ) you also, when you heard the word of truth, the gospel of your salvation, and believed in him, were sealed with the promised Holy Spirit. (Ephesians 1:13)

How happy we are to hear news of someone being rescued from a burning house or from the stormy sea. The best possible news is to know that we have been saved from the wrath and punishment that we deserve. We are brought from this danger by faith in Christ, to the safe place in God's love and favour. God, the Holy Spirit, helps us to appreciate just how wonderful the gospel of salvation is.

42. The Power of God

For I am not ashamed of the gospel, for it is the power of God for salvation to everyone who believes. (Romans 1:16)

God has immense power – power to create the universe, to make a mountain and an elephant, to control the wind and the sea.

His power is shown above all in the conversion of a sinner. When Jesus died on the cross he defeated Satan, and showed his immense power over everything, even death, evil and Satan.

His immense power draws a sinner to love and trust him.

43. The Gospel in Five Words

Christ died for the ungodly. (Romans 5:6)

This Bible verse has just five words, but what amazing good news. Everyone is a sinner, ungodly by nature. But in our weakness and sin, Christ Jesus died for us – not because we deserve it but because God decided. God is love.

44. The Debt is Paid

For I delivered to you as of first importance what I also received: that Christ died for our sins in accordance with the Scriptures. (1 Corinthians 15:3)

Our sins deserve punishment from God. Because of sin we owe God a great debt. But Jesus Christ has paid this debt for us when he died on the cross. The debt is cancelled. The price was too high for us to pay. Jesus paid for our sins with his own blood when it was shed on the cross.

45. The Lost is Found

The Son of Man came to seek and to save the lost. (Luke 19:10)

If you get lost, you feel so frightened and anxious. You do not know how to reach your destination. You need help.

The good news of the gospel is that Jesus came to seek those who are lost and lead them to their destination – God's kingdom.

Jesus told us stories about a lost sheep, a lost coin and a lost son (Luke 15). When they were found, there was great celebration.

There is great joy in heaven when a lost sinner is found by Jesus Christ.

46. Sin is Cleansed

The blood of Jesus his (God's) Son cleanses us from all sin. (1 John 1:7)

We have to regularly clean our bodies, our clothes and our homes to get rid of grime and dirt. But we cannot, by our own effort, get rid of the dirt and impurity that sin causes.

The good news of the gospel is that God cleanses us from all sin with the blood of Jesus. If we trust in Jesus, who shed his blood on the cross, we are made clean and acceptable in God's sight.

QUESTION, ANSWER AND MEMORY

17. How many persons are there in the one God?
Three persons. (Matthew 28:19)
18. Who are these three persons?
The Father, the Son and the Holy Spirit. (Matthew 28:19)
19. Who made the world?
God. (Genesis 1:31)

MEMORY VERSE 7
You are the God who sees (Genesis 16:13). Sometimes we do things and we think that nobody has seen us. But God sees everything we do. He knows even our thoughts. This should make a difference to the way we behave.

NOTE FROM THE AUTHOR

MEMORISING SCRIPTURE is a most valuable training for a child. Truths learned in youth stick with us and come back to our minds time and again. The Holy Spirit uses what we have learned and brings it back to our memory.

Jesus told his disciples 'The Helper, the Holy Spirit, whom the Father will send in my name, he will teach you all things, and bring to your remembrance, all things that I have said to you.' (John 14:26)

The Holy Spirit can only bring to our minds the things which we have already learned.

Encourage your children, not only to read God's Word regularly, but to learn individual verses from it. This will prove to be a priceless treasure to them for all of their lives.

CHILDREN ALWAYS have questions about what it means to be a Christian. Do they need a long philosophical answer? Not always – and it is simple answers to deep questions that are often the most effective.

Children of past generations were brought up with the immense benefit of learning the Shorter Catechism. A basic knowledge of Christian doctrine is vital in our day too.

Throughout this book you will find a simple summary of some of the essentials of the faith compiled as a set of questions and answers. The questions and answers will change after every two or three devotions. These are aimed at helping a young child to learn what everyone needs to know.

The learning of doctrine is not salvation but a good foundation of truth is valuable in combating false ideas which so easily divert young minds. Remember God's promise to his people. 'I will put my laws in their minds and write them on their hearts.'

Teaching the children is our responsibility. Applying that truth to the child's heart is the Lord's work.

47. Forgiveness Forever

For I will forgive their iniquity, and I will remember their sin no more. (Jeremiah 31:34)

If someone does something hurtful to us, we find it hard to forget. We often keep going back to think about the wrong done to us. God is not like us. He forgives us because of what the Lord Jesus has done on the cross. Our sin is covered — out of sight. God says he will remember it no more. Christ has dealt with it. This is good news. Micah tells us that God will cast all our sins into the depths of the sea (Micah 7:19).

48. Freedom from Slavery

So if the Son sets you free, you will be free indeed. (John 8:36)

Sin can capture our minds and hearts and make us slaves. Perhaps greed or jealousy or anger or dishonesty can hold a grip on our lives and keep us captive. Only Jesus can break these bonds and set us free from sin. This is very good news. Jesus sets us free to a new life to serve God.

49. Found not Guilty

If anyone does sin, we have an advocate with the Father, Jesus Christ the righteous. (1 John 2:1)

An advocate is a person who will speak for you to the judge in a court of law if you have done something wrong. Our judge is God and we have all done many wrong things – by our actions, our words or our thoughts. These sins deserve God's punishment. But Jesus is our 'advocate' who pleads for us.

'He is able to save to the uttermost those who draw near to God through him, since he always lives to make intercession for them' (Hebrews 7:25).

50. God's Free Gift

For the wages of sin is death, but the free gift of God is eternal life in Christ Jesus our Lord. (Romans 6:23)

The good news is that God has given us a free gift – totally undeserved – eternal life. We deserve death, but because of what the Lord Jesus has done we can receive the marvellous gift of eternal life.

Jesus told us that he came so that his people 'may have life and have it abundantly' (John 10:10).

51. God's Love

For God so loved the world that he gave his only Son, that whoever believes in him should not perish but have eternal life. (John 3:16)

This is really good news. God loved the people in the world so much that he worked out a plan to save them from death and hell and bring them to eternal life. God's Son came to this world as a baby called Jesus. He lived a perfect life and died to bear the punishment of the sins of whoever believes in him.

Look at the text above: John 3:16. Write the initial letter of word number: 2 11 12 20 23 24

– – – – – –

52. A New Creation

If anyone is in Christ, he is a new creation. (2 Corinthians 5:17)

When someone trusts in the Lord Jesus Christ, life changes. The person who was dead in sin, is made alive – a new creation. God gives him or her a new heart that wants to obey God. This is a wonderful gift from God – such good news for us.

Jesus described this changed life as being born again (John 3:7). A person has to be born again to enter the kingdom of heaven.

53. Knowledge of the Truth

God desires all people to be saved and to come to the knowledge of the truth. (1 Timothy 2:4)

Jesus is the truth. God wants us to be saved and to really know Jesus, not just know about him.

To really know Jesus and have him as our friend, we need to spend time with him, speaking to him in prayer and listening to what he has to say to us in the Scriptures, the Bible.

Just as we love spending time with our friends, we will love spending time with Jesus. What good news to know that he is our friend.

QUESTION, ANSWER AND MEMORY

20. Did God make the world out of something?
No. There was nothing else before the world. (Hebrews 11:3)
21. How did God make the world?
By speaking powerful words. (Psalm 148:5)
22. How long did it take?
Six days. (Genesis 1:1-31)

MEMORY VERSE 8
The Lord has done great things for us; we are glad (Psalm 126:3). The list of great things God has done for us has no end. We can try to count our blessings but we will not be able to tell of them all. We can only say thank you.

54. God's Grace

For by grace you have been saved through faith. And this is not your own doing; it is the gift of God, not a result of works, so that no one may boast. (Ephesians 2:8-9)

The gospel is not a privilege that we earn. It is a gift given to us because of God's grace. A way to remember the meaning of grace is:

G Gifts
R Received
A At
C Christ's
E Expense

We have done nothing to deserve God's kindness. We are saved by grace, through faith – this is not our own doing, it is the gift of God (see Ephesians 2:8).

55. The Gospel Brings Life

Our Saviour Christ Jesus, abolished death and brought life and immortality to light through the gospel. (2 Timothy 1:10)

One gift the gospel brings us is eternal life. Death was a consequence of Adam's sin in the Garden of Eden. Jesus Christ, God's Son, gained the victory over death by dying on the cross and rising again on the third day.

Jesus' obedience brought life for us – the life that God intended for Adam. All life became different. Everything is in our Saviour's control.

56. God Reigns

How beautiful upon the mountains are the feet of him who brings good news, who publishes peace, who brings good news of happiness, who publishes salvation, who says to Zion, 'Your God reigns.' (Isaiah 52:7)

The world is full of problems – war and disease and hunger in many places. There is chaos and trouble all over. But we have good news – 'your God reigns'.

God is in control. He upholds the whole universe by the word of his power (Hebrews 1:3). The whole of earth and heaven belong to him (Deuteronomy 10:14). He is the King of kings. In all events and with all people, God is working out his purposes. That should give us comfort and confidence to face the future.

57. The Gospel is Eternal

Then I (John) saw another angel flying directly overhead, with an eternal gospel to proclaim to those who dwell on earth, to every nation and tribe and language and people. (Revelation 14:6)

Many of the things we value today will be gone in a few years. The toys will be broken; the bike will be rusty; our friends might move on to a new town.

One thing we can be sure will remain constant is the Word of God. People will die. Heaven and earth will pass away. But God's Word will be forever. The gospel will last for all eternity. Those who are trusting Jesus have joy now and everlasting joy in the future.

This is good news.

58. Power and Holy Spirit

Our gospel came to you not only in word, but also in power and in the Holy Spirit and with full conviction. (1 Thessalonians 1:5)

The gospel is not just a collection of words on a page. The Word of God is not like any other book.

The words of the gospel are powerful because the Holy Spirit opens our minds and hearts to understand and receive the truth.

A Christian believes the gospel because of the work of God, the Holy Spirit, in his or her life.

59. The Gospel for all Nations

And the gospel must first be proclaimed to all nations. (Mark 13:10)

The gospel is for you, but not just for you. It is for people all over the world. Jesus told his disciples to preach the gospel to all nations.

God's Word – the gospel – is being translated into more and more languages. Missionaries are taking the gospel to many different countries.

Is there someone you can tell about the Lord Jesus?

60. The Gospel Never Changes

The word of the Lord remains forever. And this word is the good news that was preached to you. (1 Peter 1:25)

The good news of the gospel never changes. It is true for us today just as it was in the past. We know that this good news will be true in the future too, because it is the Word of God.

How thankful we should be that we have heard this good news – good news for today and every day of our lives. This helps us in times of difficulty or sadness.

QUESTION, ANSWER AND MEMORY

23. What did God do on the seventh day?
He rested and made the seventh day of the week his special day.
(Genesis 2:2)
24. Who was the first man God made?
Adam. (Genesis 5:2)

MEMORY VERSE 9
For to us a child is born, to us a son is given: and the government shall be upon his shoulder, and his name shall be called Wonderful Counsellor, Mighty God, Everlasting Father, Prince of Peace. (Isaiah 9:6). The birth of Jesus was foretold hundreds of years before it happened. The prophet Isaiah told about his mighty power, wisdom and care for his people.

61. Jesus Preached the Gospel

Jesus came into Galilee, proclaiming the gospel of God. (Mark 1:14)

Wherever Jesus went, he did good. He healed sick people, made blind people see and lame people walk.

He also preached the gospel wherever he went, telling people the good news of God's love for sinners and his plan to save them from eternal punishment. He knew he was going to die on the cross to carry out this plan.

62. The Gospel is to be Shared

Then Philip opened his mouth and ... he told him the good news about Jesus. (Acts 8:35)

When we hear good news – perhaps the birth of a baby or someone passing an exam – we want to pass it on to others.

We should want to pass on the very good news about Jesus to our friends.

Some people become missionaries and go to foreign lands to tell people about Jesus.

Faithful ministers pass on the good news of the gospel when they preach in church week by week.

63. The Gospel is to be Believed

The time is fulfilled, and the kingdom of God is at hand; repent and believe in the gospel. (Mark 1:15)

We can read the gospel. We can listen to the gospel. We can speak about the gospel.

But the really important thing is to believe the gospel – to realise what God has done for us and to thank him for sending his Son to save us. When we turn from sin and believe the gospel, we are saying 'yes' to Jesus.

64. A Jewel

The law from your mouth is more precious to me than thousands of pieces of silver and gold. (Psalm 119:72 NIV)

The gospel is a multi-faceted jewel which should fascinate us and rejoice our heart. Paul in his letter to the Philippians tells us that the most important thing in his life is 'knowing Christ Jesus'. Everything else is worthless compared to that great gift of 'gaining Christ' (Philippians 3:8).

Along with all the benefits – forgiveness of sin, eternal life, help of the Holy Spirit and many others – the Christian gains the supreme gift – Christ himself.

What good news.

Let's Think About

THE ONE TRUE GOD

65. God

The LORD delights in those who fear him, who put their hope in his unfailing love. (Psalm 147:11 NIV)

This is a big subject. Where do we start? God has no beginning and no end and is so great that our minds cannot fully grasp him. That does not mean that we should not think about him. He wants us to do that. He delights in us worshipping him. That is what we are made for.

God helps us to do this by telling us about himself in the Bible and in this little book we will look at some of the things that God has told us about himself.

66. God is a Spirit

I am the LORD and there is no other, besides me there is no God. (Isaiah 45:5)

God is a Spirit. He does not have a body like we have. We cannot see him, but he is very real. God is great and powerful – more than we can understand.

God had no beginning as we had. He has no end either. God never changes. He was and is and always will be wise, holy, true and loving.

There is only one living and true God – he is the greatest and the best.

67. The Trinity

Go therefore and make disciples of all nations, baptising them in the name of the Father and of the Son and of the Holy Spirit. (Matthew 28:19)

The Bible tells us there is only one God. It tells us of three different persons in this one God – God the Father, God the Son and God the Holy Spirit. These three persons are each God. They are equal in power and glory, but they each do different things.

QUESTION, ANSWER AND MEMORY

25. Who was the first woman that God made?
Eve. (Genesis 3:20)
26. What did God make Adam from?
The dust of the ground. (Genesis 2:7)

MEMORY VERSE 10
...You shall call his name Jesus, for he will save his people from their sins (Matthew 1:21). The name Jesus means 'Saviour'. The angel of the Lord appeared to Joseph in a dream and told him to call Mary's baby 'Jesus', because he would save his people from their sins – he would be the Saviour.

68. God the Father

(Jesus said), Pray then like this: 'Our Father in heaven, hallowed be your name.' (Matthew 6:9)

God the Father lives in heaven, but he is everywhere. God the Father chooses and calls his people to be saved. God the Father sent his Son to be the Saviour.

Jesus prayed to God the Father and taught us to pray to him too.

69. God the Son

For God so loved the world, that he gave his only Son, that whoever believes in him should not perish but have eternal life. (John 3:16)

God the Son was sent by the Father to this world. He was born to Mary and was given the name Jesus which means 'The Lord Saves'.

Jesus was a human like us, but he was also God. Because he was God and man, he was able to be the perfect sacrifice for our sins when he died on the cross.

70. God the Holy Spirit

Likewise the Spirit helps us in our weakness. For we do not know what to pray for as we ought, but the Spirit himself intercedes for us with groanings too deep for words. (Romans 8:26)

God the Holy Spirit is given to God's people by the Father and the Son, to live within them.

The Holy Spirit helps us to pray, helps us to understand the Bible, helps us to love and trust in the Lord Jesus Christ.

When someone becomes a Christian, they are 'born again' or 'born of the Spirit'. The Lord Jesus taught us this.

71. God is Infinite

Can you find out the deep things of God? Can you find out the limit of the Almighty? It is higher than heaven – what can you do? (Job 11:7-8)

There is no limit to God and his power. There is a limit to what we can do, but not with God.

There is no limit to his love. He loves with an everlasting love – no beginning and no end. Our love at best is very faint in comparison.

There is no limit to God's goodness, or wisdom or justice or truth.

God is infinite – no limits. Our minds, which are limited, find this hard to grasp, but we should believe and worship him as the infinite God.

72. God is Eternal

From everlasting to everlasting you are God. (Psalm 90:2)

We live in a certain time in history. The calendar and the clock affect our daily lives. God is not affected by time. God is eternal. He had no beginning. He has no end. He inhabits eternity which is not confined by time. With God, a day is like a thousand years, and a thousand years like a day.

God has promised eternal life to those who trust in the Lord Jesus Christ, the Saviour from sin.

73. God is Unchanging

For I the LORD do not change. (Malachi 3:6)

We are always changing. Our appearance changes as we grow older. Our tastes change. Our work changes. The seasons and the weather changes.

God never changes. He remains the same constantly. His promises never change. His plans and purposes never change.

He is the same yesterday and today and forever.

74. God is Immortal

To the King of the ages, immortal, invisible,the only God, be honour and glory forever and ever. Amen. (1 Timothy 1:17)

God is immortal because he never dies. People die, as do animals and birds and flowers and leaves. God's immortality is part of his nature.

He has given his people a gift – a soul that never dies and the promise of eternal life in heaven with himself.

QUESTION, ANSWER AND MEMORY

27. What did God make Eve from?
One of Adam's ribs. (Genesis 2:22)
28. What did God give to Adam and Eve as well as bodies?
He gave them souls that would never die. (Genesis 2:7).

MEMORY VERSE 11
I am the good shepherd. The good shepherd gives his life for the sheep (John 10:11). Jesus described himself as a good shepherd – one who would protect and guide and feed his flock of sheep – that is, the people who follow him. He gave his life for them.

75. God is Invisible

(God) who is the blessed and only Sovereign, the King of kings and Lord of lords ... whom no one has ever seen or can see. (1 Timothy 6:15-16)

God is invisible because he is a Spirit. God can see us all the time.

We cannot see the wind, but we can see the effects of the wind blowing the trees or making the sea rough.

We can see the effects of God at work in the world that he made and in the way he keeps us and provides for us.

76. God is Omnipotent/Almighty

The LORD appeared to Abram and said to him, 'I am God Almighty, walk before me, and be blameless.' (Genesis 17:1)

All power in heaven and in earth belongs to God. He alone has the power to give life and breath to every creature. The most powerful man in the world is feeble compared to the powerful God. Nobody can resist God and his purposes.

God even has power to forgive sin.

77. God is Omnipresent

'Can a man hide himself in secret places so that I cannot see him?' declares the LORD. 'Do I not fill heaven and earth?' declares the LORD. (Jeremiah 23:24)

God is omnipresent. We can be in only one place at one time. God is a Spirit. He does not have a body. He is everywhere. He fills the whole earth and heaven.

He is with us when we are awake or asleep. He is with us at home, at play, at church and at school. He is with us when we are happy or sad. There is no place at all where God is not present.

78. God is Omniscient

For he (God) knows the secrets of the heart. (Psalm 44:21)

God knows everything. He even knows the number of hairs on your head. He knows when a little bird falls to the ground. He knows how many stars are in the sky. He knows what we say, and do and think about.

God knows all things. He knows if we love him.

79. God's Work of Creation

In the beginning, God created the heavens and the earth. (Genesis 1:1)

God made the world and everything in it in six days. He made it from nothing, just by speaking his powerful word. He made the sun, the moon and all the stars. He made the day and the night. He made the birds, the fish and the animals. God formed a man called Adam from the dust of the ground and breathed life into him. God put Adam to sleep and removed one of his ribs. God created a woman called Eve from Adam's rib. God was pleased with all that he had made – his work of Creation.

80. God's Work of Providence

(God) works all things according to the counsel of his will. (Ephesians 1:11)

God's power not only made the world and everything in it, but keeps it going every day. God is the sustainer of all life. He is good and kind and in control of all things. Nothing takes him by surprise. All events in our lives happen to fulfil his purpose – even the things that we think are sad or  difficult. His ways are far above our ways. He has a plan for all his people – a plan for our good and his glory.

81. God is Holy

Holy, holy, holy is the Lord of hosts; the whole earth is full of his glory. (Isaiah 6:3)

God is completely free from sin. This means he is so different from us, because we sin in what we think, and say and do. Because God is holy, he hates sin and has to punish it. The Saviour, Jesus Christ, God's Son took the punishment for those who believe in him.

God asks his people to be holy as he is holy. This is a gradual work of God's grace – not complete until death. Because God is holy, we should worship him.

QUESTION, ANSWER AND MEMORY

29. Do you have a soul as well as a body?
Yes. I have a soul that will never die. (Matthew 16:26)
30. How do you know that you have a soul?
Because God tells me so in the Bible. (Psalm 121:7)
31. Were Adam and Eve good when God made them?
Yes, very good. All that God made was good. (Genesis 1:31)

MEMORY VERSE 12
I am the way, and the truth, and the life. No one comes to the Father except through me (John 14:6). The only way to God the Father is the Lord Jesus. Jesus is the truth of God and the life of God.

82. God is Good

For the LORD is good; his steadfast love endures forever, and his faithfulness to all generations. (Psalm 100:5)

God is good in all that he is and all that he does. He is good when he gives us so many good gifts – food, drink, shelter, family.

He is good because he keeps his promises. He is good because he gave us wise commandments to follow. He is good when he corrects us for our mistakes. He is so good to us because he gave us his Son and will graciously give us all things.

83. God is Righteous

The LORD within her is righteous; he does no injustice. (Zephaniah 3:5)

God is righteous and just. He never does wrong. He never makes a mistake. He is the Judge and all his judgements are always completely fair and just.

We do not always understand what God is doing in the world or in our lives, but we can be confident that he understands and is doing everything fairly and wisely.

84. God is Gracious

The LORD is gracious and merciful, slow to anger and abounding in steadfast love. (Psalm 145:8)

Grace is the undeserved love of God to people because of what Jesus Christ has done.

All that God does for us is because he is gracious and deals with us, not because we deserve his love and favour, but because he delights in love and mercy. He is also absolutely just and hates sin, but Jesus Christ, the Son of God has taken the punishment for the sin of his people.

If God gave us what we deserve, we would be destroyed. But God is more gracious than we can understand. How thankful we should be.

85. God is Love

God is love, and whoever abides in love abides in God and God abides in him. (1 John 4:16)

God does not only show love to his people, he is love. Love is one of his main characteristics. We may love someone who is good to us, but God loved us even when we were his enemies. His love is so great it reaches the heavens, David the psalm-writer said (Psalm 36:5).

He loved us so much that he sent his Son to die for us on the cross. There is no greater love than that. The Bible tells us that we love because God first loved us.

86. God is True

But the LORD is the true God; he is the loving God and the everlasting King. (Jeremiah 10:10)

The LORD God is the only true God. Many people in the world worship false gods, an idol of stone or a person or an idea. These false gods cannot hear or answer prayer.

God's character is true. He does not lie. All he says is the truth. We can completely rely on him and his Word.

87. God Guides

This is God, our God forever and ever. He will guide us forever. (Psalm 48:14)

When we are on a journey it is good to have a guide to point us in the right direction, so that we do not stray off the road and into danger.

Life is like a journey and God is the best guide we can have. His Word tells us how to live in obedience and love to him and how to serve and love other people.

God guides us in the things which happen from day to day.

88. God Teaches

I will instruct you and teach you in the way you should go. (Psalm 32:8)

Our teachers at school will tell us about many subjects – maths, geography, history. We have to listen and be willing to learn.

God, in his Word, teaches us about himself, about the dangers of sin, about the salvation that has been obtained for us by the Lord Jesus Christ. How important it is to pay attention and learn these valuable lessons.

God teaches us by his 'providence' in the things that happen to us day by day. Even the hard and difficult happenings teach us good lessons. God does all things well.

QUESTION, ANSWER AND MEMORY

32. What is sin?
Sin is disobeying or not keeping God's law in any way.
(Romans 5:12)
33. What is disobeying God's law?
Doing what God says not to do. (Luke 22:61)
34. What is not keeping God's law?
Not being or doing what God requires. (Luke 10:31)

MEMORY VERSE 13
I am the bread of life; whoever comes to me shall not hunger, and whoever believes in me shall never thirst (John 6:35). Every person has a longing that needs to be satisfied. This longing is like hunger or thirst. The only satisfaction for this longing is in the Lord Jesus.

89. God Corrects

The LORD reproves (or corrects) him whom he loves, as a father the son in whom he delights. (Proverbs 3:12)

When we make a mistake in a school exercise, the teacher will point out the mistake and help us to reach the correct answer.

God hates sin. When his people sin, God as a loving Father, must point out that sin and correct them. God, in his Word, confronts us with our sin and shows us the correct way to think and act. If we confess our sin, he is faithful and just to forgive us our sin.

90. God Comforts

Blessed be the God and Father of our Lord Jesus Christ, the Father of mercies and God of all comfort, who comforts us in all our affliction. (2 Corinthians 1:3-4)

If our friend is unhappy or in trouble, we sometimes do not know what to say to help them. We might say something that makes them feel worse. But God always knows how to comfort. His love is perfect. He is the God of all comfort. His words encourage and strengthen us when we are unhappy or in trouble.

'Let not your hearts be troubled,' he tells us. 'Believe in God.' The Bible is full of comforting words like that.

91. God is Forgiving

If we confess our sins, he is faithful and just to forgive us our sins and to cleanse us from all unrighteousness. (1 John 1:9)

Only God can forgive sin. He cancels the sinner's debt because Jesus Christ, God's Son, died on the cross to bear the punishment for the sin of those who repent and trust in him.

God has promised that when he forgives their iniquity, he will not remember their sin any more. Micah told us that God will cast all our sin into the depths of the sea. God delights to forgive the sinner who comes to him in faith.(Micah 7:19)

92. God is King

For God is the King of all the earth; sing praises with a psalm. (Psalm 47:7)

A king is a ruler of a kingdom and is the most important person in the country. God is the King over everyone in the world, even all the kings and queens and presidents. He is the King of kings, and Lord of lords. His kingdom will last for ever.

The Bible tells us that one day everyone in the world will bow down before him and worship.

93. God Gave His Word

All Scripture is breathed out by God and profitable for teaching, for reproof, for correction and for training in righteousness. (2 Timothy 3:16)

How we love to receive a letter or a card from someone we love. We like to know that they are thinking of us. God has sent us an amazing message – not just one letter – but in the sixty-six books of the Bible, telling us that he is thinking of us and loves us. He tells us about himself and what he has done for us. He tells us what we are to believe and what we are to do.

God's book has survived down through the centuries. 'Heaven and earth will disappear,' Jesus the Son of God said, 'but my words will remain for ever.'

94. God Gives All Things

He who did not spare his own Son, but gave him up for us all, how will he not also with him graciously give us all things? (Romans 8:32)

We all need food and clothes and a home. Our parents provide these for us, probably. But it is God who has provided, so that your needs will be met. All good gifts come from him.

Our need for love, security, and protection come first from God our Heavenly Father. He cares for us more than anyone else could. Nothing is too hard for him. He does not promise to supply everything we want, but we can depend on him to supply all our needs.

95. God's Name

I will praise the name of God with a song; I will magnify him with thanksgiving. (Psalm 69:30)

One of the commandments tells us not to take God's name in vain. We must use his name with care and reverence.

God has many special names which tell us about his character. 'Elohim' tells us that he is strong and mighty. 'Jehovah Jireh' reminds us that he provides for all our needs. 'El Elyon' means Most High.

Yahweh is a very personal, holy name which God uses with his special people. They can use the name Yahweh because God made a covenant (a special promise) with them, promising to be their faithful God.

QUESTION, ANSWER AND MEMORY

35. Did Adam and Eve continue to be good?
No. They sinned by disobeying God. (Genesis 2:17)
36. How did Adam and Eve sin?
By eating fruit that God had said not to eat. (Genesis 3:6)

MEMORY VERSE 14
I am the light of the world. Whoever follows me will not walk in darkness, but have the light of life (John 8:12). If you were out walking in the countryside on a dark night, you would need a light to show you the way and to stop you from stumbling. Jesus is the light to guide and help us in this dark sinful world.

96. We are Made to Worship God

All the ends of the earth shall remember and turn to the Lord, and all the families of the nations shall worship before you. (Psalm 22:27)

The bird is made to fly. The fish is made to swim. And we are made to worship God.

Our chief purpose in living is to serve God who made us. Everything we do should be to the glory of God – eating, drinking, playing, working. Worshipping in church is just a part of serving him.

97. Glorify God

I will praise you, Lord my God, with all my heart; I will glorify your name for ever. (Psalm 86:12 NIV)

Our chief purpose in life is to glorify God and enjoy him forever. God has revealed to us so much of his character and work in creation and providence and the Bible to help us to do this.

We will never grasp the great extent of his being, but we can enjoy the little that we do understand. We cannot see the beauty and wonder of the whole world, but we can enjoy even the view of the garden from the kitchen window or simply the little bird in the sky.

Pray now that you will see something of the wonder, majesty and glory of God. May we thank God for what he has told us about himself. Glorify and enjoy the one true God.

NOTE FROM THE AUTHOR

We all need to understand the God of the Bible. The Bible tells us so much about who God is, what he has done and what he is still doing.

There are many different aspects to God's character ... God is love, God is holy, God comforts, God guides – to name just a few.

When we understand these things then we are more able to worship God.

Now the church is just one of the places where we go to worship God but it is more than just that ... it is more than just a building. The church is a group of people that spans the whole of history. If you love and trust in God's Son, the Lord Jesus Christ, then you are also part of God's church.

Jesus Christ has promised to build his church – he adds to it daily – he cares for it more than we can understand.

Children and families need to know the truth about the church because children are not just the church of tomorrow – they are the church of today.

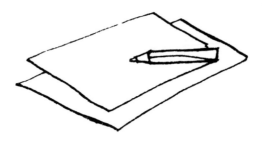

Let's Think About
THE CHURCH

98. What is the Church?

So the churches were strengthened in the faith and grew daily in numbers. (Acts 16:5 NIV)

What comes to mind when you hear the word 'church'? Perhaps you might think of a building with a spire, or a hall where services are held.

When God in his Word, speaks of the church he is referring to the people who belong to him. They meet from time to time sometimes in a building, sometimes not. The people are the church. The people are God's. He strengthens them and makes them grow spiritually. There are great privileges and blessings, responsibilities and work for the church.

99. The People of God

To the church of God that is in Corinth, to those sanctified in Christ Jesus, called to be saints together with all those who in every place call upon the name of our Lord Jesus Christ. (1 Corinthians 1:2)

So when God speaks in the Bible about the church, he is referring to those who belong to him. Where are those people? Well, the church is all over the world. It is made up of the people everywhere who call on the name of the Lord Jesus.

The church is also the group of people that meet together regularly to worship God. The Bible tells us that the church will have in it people from every language and nation. (Revelation 5:9).

100. Christian

… And when he had found him, he brought him to Antioch. For a whole year they met with the church and taught a great many people. And in Antioch the disciples were first called Christians. (Acts 11:26)

Christian is one of the names given to those who follow the Lord Jesus Christ – those who are part of the church.

Barnabas and Paul worked with the church in Antioch, preaching and teaching. There the followers of Jesus Christ were first called Christians. Only people who trust in Jesus can be called Christians.

QUESTION, ANSWER AND MEMORY

37. What happened to Adam and Eve when they sinned?
They were separated from God. (Genesis 3:24)
38. Does Adam's sin affect us?
Yes. We are all Adam's children. He acted for us all and as a result we are all born in a sinful condition. (Romans 5:12)

MEMORY VERSE 15
For I know that my Redeemer lives, and at the last he will he will stand upon the earth (Job 19:25). Job wrote these words when he was suffering very badly. He had hope and comfort in knowing that God, the redeemer, would do justly at the last day.

101. Believers

And believers were increasingly added to the Lord, multitudes of both men and women. (Acts 5:14 NKJV)

A believer is someone who believes the truth about the Lord Jesus Christ. A man once asked Paul, 'What must I do to be saved?' The answer was very simple – 'Believe on the Lord Jesus Christ and you shall be saved,' (Acts 16:31).

God, the Holy Spirit, gives the power to believe. Many people can merely know about Jesus – who he was and what he did. A true believer will have a personal relationship with Jesus and will put his trust in him.

102. Faithful

To the saints and faithful brothers in Christ at Colossae: Grace to you and peace from God our Father. (Colossians 1:2)

When Paul wrote to the church at Colossae he called them saints and faithful brothers. They did not just try to do their best to please God; they knew they could not trust their own goodness. They put all their faith and trust in the Lord Jesus Christ. They knew he had given his life for them.

The Christian who has faith in God, will be faithful to him. God is always faithful to his people, the church. Without faith it is impossible to please God, for he who comes to God must believe that he is, and that he is a rewarder of those who diligently seek him (Hebrews 11:6).

103. Family of God

... I bow my knees to the Father of our Lord Jesus Christ, from whom the whole family in heaven and earth is named (Ephesians 3:14-15 NKJV) Behold what manner of love the Father has bestowed on us, that we should be called children of God (1 John 3:1 NKJV)

God's people are described as a family. Your family is made up of parents, children, grandparents. You may also have brothers, sisters, aunts, uncles and cousins. Family has a special bond – they belong to each other.

God's people have a special family bond. They have the same heavenly Father – God. Jesus Christ is their elder brother. When Christians meet they know that they belong to the same family – they are adopted into God's family.

104. Body of Christ

And He put all things under his feet, and gave Him to be head over all things to the church, which is his body, the fullness of Him who fills all in all (Ephesians 1:22-23 NKJV). For as the body is one and has many members, but all the members of that one body, being many, are one body, so also is Christ (1 Corinthians 12:12 NKJV)

Our bodies are made up of many different limbs and organs – all with a different purpose. Our legs and feet are used for walking. With our eyes we see. We smell with our nose. We work with our hands. God's church is like a body. Each person is different and useful in his own way.

The Bible tells us that Christ is the Head of this body. Without a head a body cannot live. Without Christ, the church would not survive.

105. Bride

Husbands, love your wives, just as Christ also loved the church and gave Himself for her. (Ephesians 5:25 NKJV)

A bride and bridegroom love each other so much that they get married and live together as a family. Jesus Christ is described as the husband who loves his wife, the church, so much that he gave himself for her.

Jesus gave himself for his people, the church when he suffered and died on the cross to take the punishment due for their sins. There is no greater love than that. 'We love Him because He first loved us.' (1 John 4:19 NKJV)

The church is like a bride who has eyes only for her bridegroom. Jesus Christ is the most important person for the church.

106. Building

For we are God's fellow workers; you are God's field, you are God's building (1 Corinthians 3:9 NKJV).
You also, as living stones, are being built up a spiritual house, a holy priesthood, to offer up spiritual sacrifices acceptable to God through Jesus Christ. (1 Peter 2:5 NKJV)

A house is made up of stones and bricks skilfully put together by the builder. Christians are part of God's spiritual building — all joined to Christ who is the chief cornerstone, the most important stone which keeps the building together. Every stone in the wall of the house is necessary. Every Christian is a necessary part of Christ's church. God is the master builder of this building — the church.

107. Light of the World

You are the light of the world. A city that is set on a hill cannot be hidden. (Matthew 5:14 NKJV)

A light bulb does not produce light by itself. It only gives light if it is connected to the energy source. A Christian gives light to the world only by being connected to the Lord Jesus Christ. This light is shown by good deeds. When others see that, they will know it is because Jesus Christ is dwelling in him and they will praise God.

The reflected light in the life of a Christian will be a help and guide to others, leading them to the great source of light, the Lord Jesus Christ.

For you were once darkness, but now you are light in the Lord. Walk as children of light (Ephesians 5:8 NKJV).

QUESTION, ANSWER AND MEMORY

39. What name do we give to this sinful condition?
Original sin. (Romans 7:23)
40. What other sin are we guilty of as well as original sin?
Actual sin in what we do, say and think. (Matthew 15:19)

MEMORY VERSE 16
The Lord is my shepherd; I shall not want (Psalm 23:1). The good shepherd takes care of his sheep. He leads them to good pastures for food and quiet waters for drink. God takes care of his people too – giving them food for body and for soul.

108. Sheep

And when he brings out his own sheep, he goes before them; and the sheep follow him, for they know his voice (John 10:4 NKJV).

The church is described as a flock of sheep, with the Lord Jesus Christ as the good shepherd. Sheep recognise the voice of their shepherd and follow him to the feeding pastures. He keeps them from danger and looks after them.

A Christian listens to Jesus the good shepherd who speaks through the Bible. The Bible gives nourishment and comfort. If a Christian follows the good shepherd they will be protected from many harmful things including sin.

109. Branches of Righteousness

I am the vine, you are the branches. He who abides in Me, and I in him, bears much fruit; for without Me you can do nothing (John 15:5 NKJV).
If you keep My commandments, you will abide in My love (John 15:10 NKJV).

A branch of a tree can only live if it is attached to the trunk whose roots go down into the ground. It will not bear fruit if it is cut off.

The Christian is described by Jesus as a branch of a vine. Jesus himself is the vine. Christians are the branches. Only through Jesus will the Christian bear fruit and show in his life the fruit of the Spirit – love, joy, peace, patience, kindness, goodness, faithfulness, gentleness and self-control. God wants his people, the church, to obey his Word.

110. Salvation

Nor is there salvation in any other, for there is no other name under heaven given among men by which we must be saved (Acts 4:12 NKJV).

Jesus saves his church. The name Jesus means Saviour. The Son of God became a man. He was born in this world. He came to suffer and die as a sacrifice for sin – not his own sin (he was perfect) but for the sins of his people, the church. He loves his people so much that he died on the cross so that his people would be saved from the punishment due to them because of their sin.

Those who repent and come to God by faith, receive the great blessing of salvation.

111. Justification

... being justified freely by His grace through the redemption that is in Christ Jesus ... (Romans 3:24 NKJV). Therefore having been justified by faith, we have peace with God, through our Lord Jesus Christ (Romans 5:1 NKJV).

Jesus Christ justifies his church. When the Lord Jesus died on the cross for his people, the church, he bought the pardon for all their sins, and made them acceptable in God's sight. God no longer sees their sin, but Christ's goodness. God's people are justified, just as if they had never sinned.

They are no longer condemned by the God who hates sin, but by grace they are accepted as righteous in God's sight.

112. Adoption

Behold what manner of love the Father has bestowed on us, that we should be called children of God! Therefore the world does not know us, because it did not know Him (1 John 3:1 NKJV).

For God so loved the world that He gave His only begotten Son, that whosoever believes in Him should not perish but have everlasting life (John 3:16).

God adopts his people into his family. God's love is so gracious. Those who trust in his Son, the Lord Jesus Christ, are given the right to become his children. They are adopted into God's family. Jesus Christ is their elder brother.

These children are given a special inheritance from the Father – everlasting life with him in heaven.

113. Sanctification

To the church of God which is at Corinth, to those who are sanctified in Christ Jesus, called to be saints, with all who in every place call on the name of Jesus Christ our Lord, both theirs and ours (1 Corinthians 1:2 NKJV).

Now may the God of peace himself sanctify you completely; and may your whole spirit, soul and body be preserved blameless at the coming of our Lord Jesus Christ (1 Thessalonians 5:23 NKJV).

The church is sanctified by God. God wants his people to be holy like himself. By his grace, his people, the church learn gradually to hate sin and to stop sinning. They learn also to love and do what is right and holy. God's people are not perfect; they still do, say and think what is wrong, but God's work in their heart cleanses them from all sin. Only at death is the Christian perfect. There is no sin in heaven.

114. Correction

For whom the Lᴏʀᴅ loves He chastens, and scourges every son whom He receives (Hebrews 12:6 ɴᴋᴊᴠ).

No chastening (correction) seems to be joyful for the present, but painful; nevertheless, afterward it yields the peaceable fruit of righteousness to those who have been trained by it (Hebrews 12:11 ɴᴋᴊᴠ).

The church is corrected by God. A father will correct and discipline his child when he does wrong, because he loves him. God will correct and discipline his family too. His Word, the Bible, will point out error. Sometimes difficult happenings will make us stop and pay heed to God and his will.

Correction is not a punishment, but meant to bring the child back to a loving fellowship with the Father. No one enjoys discipline, but it is good and a blessing.

QUESTION, ANSWER AND MEMORY

41. What does every sin deserve?
God's anger and punishment. (Isaiah 59:2)
42. Can anyone go to heaven with this sinful condition?
No. Our hearts must be changed before we can be fit for heaven. (Psalm 9:17)

MEMORY VERSE 17
Then a voice came from heaven, 'You are my beloved Son, in whom I am well pleased' (Mark 1:11). After Jesus, God the Son, was baptised, God the Holy Spirit came down on him like a dove, and God the Father spoke these words from heaven.

115. Meet Together

... not forsaking the assembling of ourselves together, as is the manner of some, but exhorting one another, and so much the more as you see the Day approaching (Hebrews 10:25 NKJV).

We can worship God anywhere, even on our own, but it is good to meet together. God wants us to worship together with other Christians. This makes us stronger and encourages us to live for God. It is good to meet as often as we can, especially on the Lord's Day. This gives us fellowship with God's people locally. It also helps us to get to know other believers and to care for each other. This is honouring to God.

116. Worship

But the hour is coming, and now is, when the true worshipers will worship the Father in spirit and truth; for the Father is seeking such to worship Him. God is Spirit, and those who worship Him must worship in spirit and truth (John 4:23, 24 NKJV).

God is worthy of our worship. He is all-powerful, all-knowing, everywhere, far higher than anything we can imagine. Yet he cares for us. This will make us worship him.

We can worship him by singing or praying, thinking about him or reading, listening about him. We can worship him in church with others, or on our own. We can worship God anywhere. 'Oh come, let us worship and bow down! Let us kneel before the LORD our maker' (Psalm 95:6 NKJV).

117. Pray

... constant prayer was offered to God for him (Peter) by the church (Acts 12:5 NKJV).

Ask and it will be given to you; seek and you will find; knock and it will be opened to you (Matthew 7:7 NKJV).

When Peter was in prison the church prayed earnestly for him. God intervened and Peter was miraculously freed from prison. He made his way to where the church was meeting. The girl who came to the door to answer his knock could hardly believe her ears. She rushed to tell the others. They did not even believe her at first. At last they opened the door and saw Peter. Their prayers had been answered.

118. Read the Bible

... from childhood you have known the Holy Scriptures, which are able to make you wise for salvation through faith which is in Christ Jesus (2 Timothy 3:15 NKJV).

Search from the book of the LORD, and read: Not one of these shall fail (Isaiah 34:16 NKJV).

It is important for God's people to read God's Word, the Bible both on their own and when they meet together with others. The Bible is the Word of God. It is true. God tells us about himself. He also tells us how he wants us to behave. The Bible gives us teaching and training. It corrects us and warns us against sin. It comforts us in sorrow. It feeds our souls and draws us nearer to Jesus. 'On the next Sabbath almost the whole city came together to hear the word of God' (Acts 13:44 NKJV).

119. Listening and Learning

So then faith comes by hearing, and hearing by the word of God (Romans 10:17 NKJV).

We must listen when the Word of God is read. We must listen when a Bible story is being told or when the Bible is being explained by a preacher. We can learn more about God this way. We do not only learn at school. We learn all through life. Grown-ups need to listen and learn about God too.

After Nehemiah had rebuilt the wall of Jerusalem, the people gathered together and Ezra read the Book of the Law (the part of the Bible that they had), from morning until midday. The people were attentive (Nehemiah 8:3).

120. Preaching

How then shall they call on Him in whom they have not believed? And how shall they believe in Him of whom they have not heard? And how shall they hear without a preacher? And how shall they preach unless they are sent? (Romans 10:14-15 NKJV)
Preach the Word! Be ready in season and out of season. Convince, rebuke, exhort with all longsuffering and teaching (2 Timothy 4:2 NKJV).

God has chosen some men to be preachers of his Word. A preacher proclaims the Good News about Jesus Christ by explaining what the Bible says. This is called a sermon. The preaching of God's Word is a powerful way of showing people that they are sinners. It points them to trust in Christ for salvation. A sermon will give comfort to a Christian, encourage him to be holy and happy in his heart.

121. Praising

... speaking to one another in psalms and hymns and spiritual songs, singing and making melody in your heart to the Lord (Ephesians 5:19 NKJV). After Peter preached on the day of Pentecost, thousands were added to the church. They met together in the temple every day, 'praising God and having favour with all the people' (Acts 2:47).

God's people praise him because he is so great and wonderful. We can worship God by singing psalms and hymns about him and to him. 'Come into his presence with singing,' says Psalm 100. 'I will sing of steadfast love and justice to you, O LORD, I will make music' said David in Psalm 101. God is pleased to hear his people making a joyful noise to him. Paul and Silas sang praises to God even when they were in chains in the prison.

QUESTION, ANSWER AND MEMORY

43. What did God do to save his people from his anger and punishment?
He sent his Son so that whoever believes in him would not perish but have everlasting life. (John 3:16)

MEMORY VERSE 18
For when we were still without strength, in due time Christ died for the ungodly (Romans 5:6 NKJV). Jesus Christ died for his people – those who were weak and sinful. This is the good news of the gospel.

122. Offering

So let each one give as he purposes in his heart, not grudgingly or of necessity; for God loves a cheerful giver (2 Corinthians 9:7 NKJV).

God's people give some of their money for God's work. It is used to take care of the building or to pay the wages of church workers. Some may be sent to missionaries or to people in need. This money is actually given to God and should be given cheerfully – not with a grudge or merely out of duty.

Jesus noticed a poor woman putting two small coins into the collection box. Many rich people put in large sums of money. 'She has put in more than the others,' Jesus said. 'They all put in out of their abundance, but she out of her poverty, put in all that she had, her whole livelihood' (Mark 12:43-44 NKJV).

123. Baptism

Peter said to them, 'Repent, and let every one of you be baptized in the name of Jesus Christ for the remission of sins; and you shall receive the gift of the Holy Spirit. For the promise is to you and to your children, and to all who are afar off, as many as the Lord our God will call.' ...Then those who gladly received his word were baptized; and that day about three thousand souls were added to them (Acts 2:38, 39, 41 NKJV).

Baptism is when water is applied in the name of God the Father, God the Son, and God the Holy Spirit. It is an outward sign that shows we need cleansing by the blood of Jesus Christ and that we belong to God's family. Baptism does not cleanse us from sin. Only God can do that.

124. The Lord's Supper

And as they were eating, Jesus took bread, blessed and broke it, and gave it to the disciples and said, 'Take, eat; this is My body.' Then He took the cup, and gave thanks, and gave it to them, saying, 'Drink from it, all of you. For this is My blood of the new covenant, which is shed for many for the remission of sins' (Matthew 26:26–28 NKJV).

When Christians meet together at church they sometimes have the Lord's Supper. This is also called Communion. Those who love the Lord Jesus will eat some bread and drink a little wine from a cup. Jesus did this with his disciples before he died. His followers do the same to remember his death. The broken bread is a reminder to us of his body suffering for his people. The poured-out wine reminds us of his blood shed for his people.

125. Fellowship

And they continued steadfastly in the apostles' doctrine and fellowship, in the breaking of bread, and in prayers (Acts 2:42 NKJV).

So continuing daily with one accord in the temple, and breaking bread from house to house, they ate their food with gladness and simplicity of heart (Acts 2:46).

People who love the Lord Jesus have a special bond with each other. They enjoy spending time together and talking about the Lord Jesus and the teaching of the Bible. This special friendship is called fellowship. One of the signs that someone is a Christian is to have love for other Christians.

126. Church Leaders

Let the elders who rule well be counted worthy of double honour, especially those who labour in the word and doctrine (1 Timothy 5:17 NKJV).

Every church group has leaders who take decisions about the work of the church. The pastor and elders help the people to know what the Bible says and to do what is right.

The Bible says that these men must lead godly lives themselves so that they can guide and correct others.

The pastor (or minister) has the added duty of preaching God's Word.

127. Bearing Fruit

But the fruit of the Spirit is love, joy, peace, longsuffering, kindness, goodness, faithfulness, gentleness, self-control. Against such there is no law (Galatians 5:22-23 NKJV).

If someone loves the Lord Jesus and is a member of his church, it should be obvious in the way he behaves.

When God the Holy Spirit is working in someone's life, then the fruit of the Spirit is produced. The fruit of the Spirit is love, joy, peace, patience, kindness, goodness, faithfulness, gentleness and self-control.

128. Witnessing

Then Philip opened his mouth, and beginning at this Scripture, preached Jesus to him (Acts 8:35 NKJV).

A witness is someone who tells what he has seen or heard. Someone who knows the Lord Jesus needs to tell others about him. Philip told the good news about Jesus to the Ethiopian man he met on the road. He became a believer too.

Living a Christian life is a powerful witness to others who live and work with us. The Christian who has been saved by the Lord Jesus will want to tell others that 'Jesus is Lord'.

QUESTION, ANSWER AND MEMORY

44. Who is God's Son?
The Lord Jesus Christ. (Luke 1:35)
45. How did he come to this world?
He was born in Bethlehem in a stable. (Luke 2:4-7)
46. Who was his mother?
The virgin Mary. (Matthew 1:18)

MEMORY VERSE 19
Behold! The Lamb of God, who takes away the sin of the world! (John 1:29 NKJV). John spoke these words when he saw Jesus coming towards him. They would remind the people of the lamb that was used in sacrifice. This gave a hint that Jesus would one day be offered as the sacrifice for sin.

129. Belong to Jesus Christ

... praising God and having flavour with all the people. And the Lord added to the church daily those who were being saved (Acts 2:47 NKJV).

The church belongs to Jesus Christ. He is the one who builds it. Every day people come to trust in Jesus and so become part of the church of Jesus Christ.

The church does not belong to us nor to the minister, but to Jesus because he gave his life for it. He died and rose again to provide forgiveness of sin, salvation and eternal life for his people, the CHURCH.

Let's Think About

JESUS

BIRTH AND CHILDHOOD

130. Jesus and Children

And this is eternal life, that they may know You, the only true God, and Jesus Christ whom You have sent. (John 17:3 NKJV)

Jesus has a great care for children, 'Let the children come to me,' he told his disciples. 'Don't forbid them.' Jesus wants children today to come to him. Those with a responsibility for children should do all they can to tell them about Jesus the Saviour. Pray that you will learn about Jesus as you study God's Word. He is the Son of God.

131. God and Man

In the beginning was the Word, and the Word was with God, and the Word was God. (John 1:1)

Jesus Christ is God the Son from all eternity. He is also called the Word of God. He became a man, born into this world, but he never stopped being God the Son. This is an amazing mystery for us to believe and cause us to worship.

132. Jesus' Mother

Behold, the virgin shall be with child, and bear a son, and they shall call his name Immanuel, which is translated, 'God with us'. (Matthew 1:23 NKJV)

Jesus' birth was unique. He had a human mother, Mary. She conceived the baby, Jesus, by the power of God the Holy Spirit. The special name 'Immanuel' means 'God with us.' Jesus was truly a human like us, but he was also truly God.

133. Jesus' Birth

And she (Mary) gave birth to her firstborn son and wrapped him in swaddling cloths, and laid him in a manger, because there was no room for them in the inn. (Luke 2:7)

Jesus' birth was in very humble surroundings. Mary and her husband Joseph could not find shelter at the inn. Jesus' first bed was the animals' feeding trough.

NOTE FROM THE AUTHOR

Children want to know about Jesus. They flocked to him in the past and still do today. The Scriptures that we read here show us that Jesus is throughout all Scripture. Remember that Jesus Christ is the same yesterday, today and forever. Encourage your children to make friends with the Friend of sinners, the Saviour of the world and the Lord of glory. Pray that they will find a true and eternal relationship with Jesus Christ.

134. Mary's Husband

You shall call his name Jesus, for he will save his people from their sins. (Matthew 1:21)

Joseph, Mary's husband, was a good man. An angel spoke to him in a dream and told him to call the baby JESUS, which means Saviour. All sinful thoughts, words and deeds deserve God's punishment. Jesus would take that punishment himself and so be a Saviour for his people.

135. Angels and Shepherds

And the angel said to them (the shepherds), '… For unto you is born this day in the city of David a Saviour, who is Christ the Lord.'… And they went with haste and found Mary and Joseph, and the baby lying in the manger. (Luke 2:10, 11, 16)

The angels told some ordinary shepherds at their work the wonderful news about the birth of Jesus Christ, the Saviour promised long ago. They rushed to see him and then passed on the good news to everyone they met.

136. Gifts for a King

When they (the wise men) had come into the house, they saw the young child with Mary his mother, and fell down and worshipped Him. They presented gifts to Him: gold, frankincense and myrrh. (Matthew 2:11 NKJV)

Gold is a gift fit for a king. Jesus is a king who rules over his people. Frankincense is a perfume used by priests. Jesus is our great Priest, who sacrificed himself for us and always prays for us.

Myrrh was ointment used to anoint dead bodies. Jesus came to this world to die for his people.

~~~~~~~~~~~~~~~~~

QUESTION, ANSWER AND MEMORY

47. Did he have an earthly father?
No. He came into the world by the power of the Holy Spirit. (Matthew 1:18)
48. Why did he come in this way?
So that he would be free from original sin. (Hebrews 7:26)

MEMORY VERSE 20
As far as the east is from the west, so far does he removed our transgressions from us (Psalm 103:12). The distance between north and south can be measured between the North and South poles. But the distance between east and west can never be measured. When we travel west we can still go even further west. This is a picture of the immeasurable distance that God puts between us and our sins.

137. The Passover

When He (Jesus) was twelve years old, they went up to Jerusalem according to the custom of the feast. (Luke 2:42 NKJV)

The special feast that Jesus attended was the Passover feast. This celebrated the night when the Israelites in Egypt painted lambs' blood on their door posts. The 'angel of death' then passed over their homes and the Israelites were saved. This event points to the greater salvation when Jesus shed his blood on the cross for sinners.

138. Obedience

Jesus increased in wisdom and stature, and in favour with God and men. (Luke 2:52 NKJV)

Jesus showed obedience to his parents and obedience to God. He had no sin and so never did, said or thought wrong things like we do.

If we have faith in Jesus Christ, not only is our sin forgiven, but we are accepted by God not because we are good, but because Jesus was good for us.

MIRACLES

139. Forgives Sins

When Jesus saw their faith, he said to the paralytic, 'Son, your sins are forgiven.' (Mark 2:5)

Jesus has power to forgive sins because he is God. The teachers of the law were right when they said only God can forgive sins. To prove his power and authority over sin, Jesus also healed the man's body. He was able to get up and walk.

140. Authority

And when the sun was setting, all those who had any that were sick with various diseases brought them to him (Jesus); and he laid hands on every one of them and healed them. (Luke 4:40)

At the end of a busy day preaching and teaching, Jesus still took time to help sick and needy people. Jesus has power over illness because he is God.

Jesus has power and authority over all creation. He has power over death and sin. There is no one more powerful than the one true God: God the Father, Son and Holy Spirit.

99

141. Willing and Able

A man with leprosy came to Jesus and begged him on his knees, 'If you are willing, you can make me clean.' (Mark 1:40 NIV)

A person with leprosy had to leave his home and family because the disease was so dreadful. Nobody wanted to go near a leper. Jesus showed great kindness to this man by reaching out and touching him. Jesus was not only willing, but able to heal him from the terrible disease.

142. Creator

And he awoke and rebuked the wind and said to the sea, 'Peace! Be still!' And the wind ceased, and there was a great calm. (Mark 4:39)

God created everything with a word – God created the wind and the sea with a word. Jesus (who is God the Son) spoke to the wind and the sea that he had created and they obeyed him.

143. Power Over Death

He (Jesus) took the child by the hand, and said to her, '... 'Little girl, I say to you, arise.' Immediately the girl arose and walked. (Mark 5:41-42 NKJV)

Jesus, the Creator of life, had power to restore life to the little girl. He has power even over death because he is God.

Things to Do

Remember to pray to God every day. You can use this little word to remind you how to pray to God – ACTS.

Adoration – Mention to God something wonderful about him. Give praise to God for the great things he does. **Confession** – Tell God you are sorry for your sins. Apologise and ask him to help you stay away from those sins in the future. **Thanks** – Say thank you to God for the wonderful things he does for you and gives to you. **Supplication** – This is a big word that means – Ask. There are things you need and want. You can ask God for them. He loves to answer your prayers. But remember God sometimes says Yes, sometimes No and sometimes Wait.

QUESTION, ANSWER AND MEMORY

49. Did Jesus ever commit any sin?
No. He obeyed God perfectly always. (Hebrews 4:15)
50. Why was God's Son given the name Jesus?
Jesus means Saviour and he saves his people from their sins. (Matthew 1:21)

MEMORY VERSE 21
For the wages of sin is death, but the gift of God is eternal life in Christ Jesus our Lord (Romans 6:23 NKJV). Wages are earned. Death is what we earn or deserve because of our sin. God does not give his people what they earn – he gives them the wonderful undeserved gift of eternal life because of the work of our Saviour, Jesus Christ.

144. Power Over Evil

They came to Jesus, and found the man from whom the demons had departed, sitting at the feet of Jesus, clothed and in his right mind. (Luke 8:35 NKJV)

The man had lots of evil spirits from Satan living in him which made him behave in a strange way. People were afraid of him. When Jesus healed him, there was a big change in his behaviour. Jesus is more powerful than Satan because He is God.

145. Fed The Hungry

He (Jesus) took the five loaves and two fish, and looking up to heaven, He blessed and broke and gave the loaves to the disciples; and the disciples gave them to the multitudes. (Matthew 14:19 NKJV)

Jesus is concerned about every detail of our lives. He did not want the people to go away hungry. He has power to provide all that we need, because he is God.

146. Power Over All Creation

His mother (Mary) said to the servants at the wedding, 'Whatever he says to you, do it.' (John 2:5 NKJV)

Mary knew that Jesus was the Son of God. When the servants obeyed Jesus, the water in the big pots was changed into wine. Jesus has power over all creation because he is God.

TEACHING

147. Eternal Life

He (Jesus) said to them, 'I must preach the kingdom of God to the other cities also, because for this purpose I have been sent.' (Luke 4:43 NKJV).

Jesus performed many amazing miracles – healing people, making blind men see, making water into wine, stilling the sea and lots more – but everywhere he went he wanted to preach about God and his kingdom.

Sinners need to hear the good news of Jesus Christ. It is only through trusting in him and his death on the cross, that we can be given eternal life.

THINGS TO DO

Try to learn as many of the memory verses as you can. How many can you recite right now?

148. Repent

Jesus began to preach and to say, 'Repent, for the kingdom of heaven is at hand.' (Matthew 4:17 NKJV)

Jesus tells us to repent — that is to turn from our sinful ways with sorrow and to turn to God wanting to love and serve him. Repentance is a gracious gift from our merciful God.

149. Teaching

When Jesus had ended these sayings, the people were astonished at His teaching, for He taught them as one having authority. (Matthew 7:28-29 NKJV)

The people who heard Jesus speak knew that he spoke with great power. He is the mighty Lord. People knew by his words that he was in charge.

150. Parables

And when a great multitude had gathered, and they had come to Him from every city, He spoke by a parable, 'A sower went out to sow his seed...' (Luke 8:4-5 NKJV)

A parable is a story about everyday activities. Jesus told many parables to the people. These stories had hidden meanings about God's kingdom. Only those who trusted and believed in God would understand their true meaning. We need to ask God to save us from our sin and to reveal the truth to us in the Bible.

QUESTION, ANSWER AND MEMORY

51. How did Jesus save his people from their sin?
Jesus Christ suffered and died in the place of his people to pay
the price for all their sins. (Hebrews 9:28)
52. For whom did Jesus suffer and die?
For all the people that God the Father gave him. (John 6:44-45)

MEMORY VERSE 22
Wash me thoroughly from my iniquity, and cleanse me from my sin
(Psalm 51:2 NKJV). Sin makes our lives black and dirty in God's sight.
Only he can wash us and make us clean – not with soap and water –
but with the precious blood of Jesus shed for us on Calvary's cross.

151. Ten Commandments

Jesus replied, 'Love the Lord your God with all your heart, with all your soul, and with all your mind.' This is the first and greatest commandment. And the second is like it. 'Love your neighbour as yourself.' (Matthew 22:37-39 NIV)

Jesus sums up the Ten Commandments with one word — love. If we love God with all our being then we will worship only him, not idols. We will give honour to his name and keep his day holy.

Loving others is shown by honouring our parents, and caring for the life, purity and property of others. We will also be truthful and content.

PRAYER

152. Jesus' Prayer For Believers

I pray for those who will believe in me through their word; that they all may be one, as you, Father, are in me, and I in you. (John 17:20-21 NKJV)

Jesus prayed often to his Father but these prayers are not recorded for us. John in his Gospel tells us one of Jesus' prayers. He prays for himself, he prays for his disciples and he prays for all believers through the centuries until today. He prays that we will be united in him.

153. Jesus' Prayer for the Disciples

He (Jesus) went out to the mountain to pray, and continued all night in prayer to God. (Luke 6:12 NKJV)

Jesus had twelve special disciples whom he chose from his followers. Before he chose them, he prayed all night to God his Father. He knew it was an important decision. We should also pray to God before making decisions. God has promised to help and guide us.

154. Jesus Prays on His Own

He went up on the mountain by himself to pray. When evening came, he was there alone. (Matthew 14:23)

After feeding the five thousand, Jesus sent the crowds away. He told the disciples to sail across the lake, then he went to be alone, to pray to God his Father. Prayer is important. Jesus recognised this. We need to speak to God our Father. We need to ask him to forgive us for our sins, to help us in our daily lives. But we also need to thank him and tell him that we love him.

155. Jesus Prays in the Morning

Very early in the morning while it was still dark, Jesus got up, left the house and went to a solitary place, where he prayed. (Mark 1:35 NIV)

Jesus got up early in the morning so that he could get peace to pray to his Father. Crowds of people were looking for him, but he went on to another town to preach. It is important to pray to God, one to one. We need peace and quiet to talk to our Heavenly Father. We need to say sorry for the bad things in our lives. We need to ask God for his strength to defeat sin.

SON OF GOD/SON OF MAN

156. We Need Salvation

For the Son of Man has come to seek and to save that which was lost. (Luke 19:10 NKJV)

We all need God's salvation. We all disobey God's law and do wrong things. Jesus is powerful enough to change us because he is God. He died to take the punishment for our sins.

157. Jesus The Sacrifice

John (the Baptist) said, 'Behold! The Lamb of God who takes away the sin of the world!' (John 1:29 NKJV)

John was pointing to Jesus the Saviour. Jesus died on the cross as a sacrifice for the sins of his people. If we have faith in Jesus, he will take away our sin and make us clean in God's sight.

QUESTION, ANSWER AND MEMORY

53. Who will be saved?
Only those who repent of their sins and believe in Jesus Christ.
(Mark 1:15)
54. What does it mean to repent of your sin?
I am truly sorry for my sins. I hate them and want to stop doing them. I want to live to please God. (Isaiah 1:16-17)

MEMORY VERSE 23
Come now, and let us reason together, says the Lord, though your sins are like scarlet, they shall be as white as snow, though they are red like crimson, they shall be as wool (Isaiah 1:18 NKJV). Our sins are described as being scarlet or crimson – bright red in colour. But God's promise of forgiveness is like the pure white snow and the soft white wool. What a contrast!

158. Peter's Faith

Simon Peter answered, 'Lord, to whom shall we go? You have the words of eternal life. Also we have come to believe and know that You are the Christ, the Son of the living God.' (John 6:68-69 NKJV)

Peter knew that Jesus is the one that we can safely trust. Peter showed that he had faith in Jesus, the Holy One of God. It is only through Jesus that we can go to heaven when we die.

159. God's Gift

For God so loved the world that He gave His only begotten Son, that whoever believes in Him should not perish, but have everlasting life. (John 3:16 NKJV)

God has given us many gifts, but the greatest one of all is the gift of his Son who came to this world as a man and willingly gave his life for us on the cross at Calvary. Jesus died in our place. If we trust in the Lord Jesus, we have eternal life.

160. Jesus' Baptism

A voice came from heaven, 'You are My beloved Son, in whom I am well pleased.' (Mark 1:11 NKJV)

When Jesus was baptised in the River Jordan, the Spirit of God came down on him in the form of a dove. God the Father spoke from heaven. He was pleased with Jesus, God the Son. The Bible tells us that the Father is God, the Son is God, and the Spirit is God. The Bible also tells us that these three persons form only one God.

161. Jesus' Humility

Jesus said, 'Foxes have holes and birds of the air have nests, but the Son of Man has nowhere to lay his head.' (Matthew 8:20)

Jesus was born in a humble condition. He was poor. He did not own a house or have lots of money. Yet he is the Creator of the whole earth. He is the King of kings and Lord of lords. He became poor so that one day his people would have the riches and treasures of eternal life.

~~~~~~~~~~

PUZZLE TIME

Over the next few pages you will be finding out about different names and descriptions of Jesus. The words in bold are back to front. Rearrange the letters so you can discover these names of Jesus...

the **daerb** of **efil**

the **thgil** of the **dlrow**

the **doog drehpehs**

the **yaw**, the **hturt** and the **efil**

the **rood**

the **eniv**

the **noitcerruser** and the **efil**

162. Bread

(Jesus said), 'I am the bread of life. Whoever comes to Me shall never hunger, and he who believes in Me shall never thirst.' (John 6:35 NKJV)

Everyone has a longing that needs to be satisfied. This longing is like hunger or thirst. Our spirits or souls long for something that the world cannot give us. Money cannot buy satisfaction. Friends and family can't give it to us. The only satisfaction for this longing is in the Lord Jesus Christ.

163. Light

(Jesus said), 'I am the light of the world. He who follows Me shall not walk in darkness, but have the light of life.' (John 8:12 NKJV)

Jesus as the light gives us guidance and leading. He clears away the darkness of evil. Jesus' light shows up our own sins and helps us to see him as our Saviour who takes away our sin.

164. Shepherd

(Jesus said), 'I am the good shepherd. The good shepherd gives His life for the sheep.' (John 10:11 NKJV)

Jesus loves and cares for all those who follow him. He provides for their needs just as a good shepherd looks after his sheep. He loves his people so much that he even gave his life for them.

QUESTION, ANSWER AND MEMORY

55. Can you decide to repent and believe in Jesus on your own?
No. I can only do so with the help of the Holy Spirit. (Romans 2:4)
56. How can you get the Holy Spirit's help?
By praying to God to give me his help. (Luke 11:13)

MEMORY VERSE 24
I have not come to call the righteous, but sinners, to repentance (Luke 5:32). The people who think they are good, do not see their need of a Saviour. Those who know they are sinners are called to repent by God. To repent means to turn from sin and to be truly sorry for it.

165. Truth

Jesus said, 'I am the way, the truth and the life. No one comes to the Father except through Me.' (John 14:6 NKJV)

There is only one way to come to God and to be in heaven at last. That way is through the Lord Jesus Christ. All that Jesus says is true because he is truth. He is Creator of life and keeps us in life. Through him we can have eternal life in heaven. Those who trust in Jesus and believe that he is the only one who can save people from their sin, will one day be in heaven with Jesus forever.

166. Door

Jesus said, 'I am the door. If anyone enters by Me, he will be saved.' (John 10:9 NKJV)

To enter a room, we go through the door. Only through Jesus do we have access to God the Father, and have salvation from our sins.

167. Vine

(Jesus said), 'I am the vine, you are the branches. He who abides in Me, and I in him, bears much fruit.' (John 15:5 NKJV)

The branch which bears the grapes depends on the vine tree. If it is cut off from the vine it will die. Those who trust in Jesus depend on him for nourishment and life. A fruitful vine grows grapes. A fruitful Christian will show love, joy and peace.

168. Life

Jesus said, 'I am the resurrection and the life. He who believes in Me, though he may die, he shall live.' (John 11:25 NKJV)

Jesus has power over life and death. He rose from the dead and at the resurrection day believers will be raised up by him, to everlasting life.

169. The Lord's Supper

Jesus took bread, blessed and broke it, and gave it to the disciples saying, 'Take, eat, this is My body.' (Matthew 26:26 NKJV)

The Lord's Supper is still celebrated in Christian churches. The broken bread tells about Jesus' body which was crucified for his people and the poured out wine tells of his blood which was shed for sinners.

170. Gethsemane

Then Jesus came with them (his disciples) to a place called Gethsemane, and he said to them, 'Sit here while I go and pray over there.' (Matthew 26:36 NKJV)

Jesus and his disciples often met in the garden of Gethsemane. Jesus was very sad. He knew what great suffering he would soon have when the anger of God was poured out on him. Jesus willingly took this anger on himself to save his people from suffering it.

171. Golgotha

They brought Him (Jesus) to the place called Golgotha... and they crucified Him. (Mark 15:22,25 NKJV)

Jesus' suffering and death were part of a wonderful plan of salvation for his people. All sin deserves to be punished. Jesus took the full weight of the just anger of God on himself so that those who trust in him would be saved. Are you trusting in him?

QUESTION, ANSWER AND MEMORY

57. How were people saved who lived before Christ died?
They believed in the Saviour that God would send. (Romans 4:3)
58. In what different ways did Jesus fulfil Old Testament promises about himself?
He came to be a prophet, a priest and a king. (Acts 3:22. Hebrews 5:6. Psalm 2:6)

MEMORY VERSE 25
For God so loved the world that He gave His only begotten Son, that whoever believes in Him should not perish but have everlasting life (John 3:16 NKJV). This verse sums up the good news of the gospel. God gave the best gift – his only Son, Jesus. Whoever believes in him and trusts in what he has done, will have the privilege of everlasting life with him in heaven.

172. Forgiveness

Jesus said, 'Father, forgive them, for they do not know what they are doing.' (Luke 23:34 NIV)

Even in the middle of his sufferings, Jesus prayed for those who were hurting him. He asked God to forgive them. What love he showed to his enemies! We should understand that we need forgiveness.

173. Jesus is Lord

Jesus cried out with a loud voice, and breathed His last. (Mark 15:37 NKJV)

When the centurion, who stood opposite Jesus, heard his cry and saw how he died, he said, 'Truly this man was the Son of God.' (Mark 15:39 NKJV).The soldiers who witnessed Jesus' death were afraid. They were convinced that Jesus was truly the Son of God. The Bible says that one day every knee shall bow and every tongue shall confess that Jesus Christ is Lord.

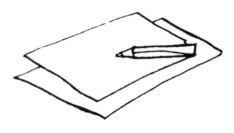

174. Jesus Was Dead

So Joseph (of Arimathea) bought some linen cloth, took down the body, wrapped it in the linen and placed it in a tomb cut out of rock. (Mark 15:46 NIV)

Joseph was a wealthy man who owned a burial place cut into the rock. The tomb was then sealed with a large round stone slab across the entrance. Jesus was definitely dead. He wasn't pretending. He had died just as God had planned. But God's plan didn't end there.

RESURRECTION/ASCENSION

175. Jesus is Alive

The angel said to the women, 'Do not be afraid, for I know that you are looking for Jesus, who was crucified. He is not here; he has risen.' (Matthew 28:5-6 NIV)

The Lord Jesus Christ conquered death. His body did not remain in the tomb. When the women came to see the tomb, the stone had been rolled away. Jesus was no longer there. He was alive again. Sin and death had been conquered. Jesus showed God's power. There is no one more powerful than the one true God.

176. Eye Witnesses

While they (the disciples) were still talking, Jesus himself stood among them and said to them, 'Peace be with you.' (Luke 24:36 NIV)

Jesus appeared to many people after he rose from the dead. He came to the room where the disciples were meeting. They were frightened because they thought he was a ghost. He reassured them that he was really alive. He told them to touch him to make sure. Are you one of those who believe in Jesus' resurrection?

177. The Ascension

While he blessed them, he parted from them and was carried up into heaven. (Luke 24:51)

Jesus' body was taken up into heaven while the disciples watched. They worshipped him because he is God. They were filled with joy, praising and blessing God.

178. Jesus Will Come Back

This same Jesus, who was taken up from you into heaven, will so come in like manner as you saw Him go into heaven. (Acts 1:11 NKJV)

God tells us that Jesus will come back to this earth. Everybody will bow before Jesus one day – either in judgement or trusting in him by his gracious mercy. For God is truly gracious – because he loves us and offers salvation to his people who don't deserve his goodness.

QUESTION, ANSWER AND MEMORY

59. How is Christ our prophet?
He teaches us the will of God. (John 16:13)
60. How is Christ our priest?
We are guilty of sin and he has died as a sacrifice for the sins of his people. Now that he has risen and ascended, he continually prays for them. (Colossians 1:20)

MEMORY VERSE 26
But God demonstrates his own love toward us, in that while we were still sinners, Christ died for us (Romans 5:8 NKJV). Christ died to save sinners. We must come to him as sinners. We do not have to prove that we are even a little bit good. Christ has taken our place.

179. Jesus the Priest

We have a great high priest, who has passed into the heavens, Jesus the Son of God. (Hebrews 4:14 NKJV)

A priest offers a sacrifice for the sins of the people. Jesus offered himself as the perfect sacrifice once and for all. A priest also prays for the people. Jesus in heaven is praying continually for his people.

180. Jesus the Saviour

Nor is there salvation in any other, for there is no other name under heaven given among men by which we must be saved. (Acts 4:12 NKJV)

Jesus Christ is the only way to God. Because he died and rose again, he is the Saviour for all who trust in him.

181. Jesus the Peacemaker

For there is one God and one Mediator between God and men, the man Christ Jesus. (1 Timothy 2:5 NKJV)

Jesus is the only one who can make peace between a holy God and sinful men. He is both God and man. He became one of us and took our punishment. He never stopped being God. God the Father accepted his sacrifice for us.

PUZZLE TIME

Go back through the pages in this book to find some Bible verses. Where does it say in the Bible that Jesus

1. Is Our High Priest?

2. Is God's only Son?

3. Was born of a Virgin?

4. Grew in wisdom?

5. Has authority over nature?

6. Prays for others?

182. Jesus is Exalted

God has exalted Jesus to his right hand to be Prince and Saviour, to give repentance to Israel and forgiveness of sins. (Acts 5:31 NKJV)

Jesus our Saviour is now exalted in heaven, sitting at God's right hand. Among his gifts to his people are repentance and forgiveness for all our sins.

183. Jesus Prays for His People

Therefore He is able to save to the uttermost those who come to God through Him, since he always lives to make intercession for them. (Hebrews 7:25 NKJV)

Sometimes we forget to pray for ourselves, but Jesus never forgets to pray for his people. He is always praying for them every day. That's what the word 'intercession' means.

184. Jesus is with Us

(Jesus said), 'I am with you always, even to the end of the age.' (Matthew 28:20 NKJV)

One of Jesus' names is Immanuel – 'God with us.' Jesus promised to be with his people always. If you trust him, he is with you today and forever. He will never leave you.

185. The Gospel

These are written that you may believe that Jesus is the Christ, the Son of God, and that believing you may have life in His name. (John 20:31 NKJV)

The Gospel has been given to us by God so that we would come to know the Lord Jesus Christ and believe in him. Believing in him is the only way for us to be saved from sin and live a worthwhile life.

186. Do You Believe?

Now we believe, not because of what you said, for we ourselves have heard Him and we know that this is indeed the Christ, the Saviour of the world. (John 4:42 NKJV)

Some Samaritan people heard how one lady had met Jesus and he had changed her life. They heard Jesus themselves and then they believed that he was the Christ, the Saviour of the world. You have also heard about Jesus. Do you believe in him? Is he your Saviour?

QUESTION, ANSWER AND MEMORY

61. How is Christ our king?
He rules the world and defends his people from Satan, the evil one. (2 Corinthians 10:5)
62. How many commandments did God give on Mount Sinai?
Ten commandments. (Exodus 20:3-17)

MEMORY VERSE 27
For by grace you have been saved through faith, and that not of yourselves, it is the gift of God (Ephesians 2:8 NKJV). The gift of salvation from God comes to us by grace – we do not deserve it – we cannot pay him back. We receive it through faith – by trusting wholly in him.

Let's Think About

BIBLE

PROMISES

GOD CARES

187. Reliable

There has not failed one word of all His (God's) good promise. (1 Kings 8:56 NKJV)
He who promised is faithful. (Hebrews 10:23 NKJV)

In the Bible we read many promises that God has given to his people. God never breaks a promise. He never forgets what he has promised. God's promises are always reliable.

188. The Universe

While the earth remains, seedtime and harvest, cold and heat, winter and summer, and day and night shall not cease. (Genesis 8:22 NKJV)

God has promised the order of the seasons every year. He has promised the day and the night in each twenty-four hour period. God is in control of the whole universe.

189. The Rainbow

I set My rainbow in the cloud and it shall be for the sign of the covenant between Me and the earth: ... the waters shall never again become a flood to destroy all flesh. (Genesis 9:13, 15 NKJV) But the day of the Lord will come like a thief, and then the heavens will pass away with a roar, and the heavenly bodies will be burned up and dissolved, and the earth and the works that are done on it will be exposed. (2 Peter 3:10)

The rainbow is a reminder of God's promise that he will never destroy the world again by water. He has, however, promised that one day he will destroy this world with fire.

190. God Will Never Leave

For He (God) Himself has said, 'I will never leave you nor forsake you.' (Hebrews 13:5 NKJV)

What a comfort to know that God is always with us. Our dearest family member or closest friend will have to leave us one day, but God will always be with his children.

191. God Will Keep You

Behold, I am with you and will keep you wherever you go. (Genesis 28:15 NKJV)

God spoke this promise first to Jacob but it is true for all who believe in him. Wherever you go, God will keep you.

192. God Provides

And my God shall supply all your need according to His riches in glory by Christ Jesus. (Philippians 4:19 NKJV)

All that we have comes from God. His provision for us of food, clothing, friends, family and lots more shows his wonderful love and blessing.

QUESTION, ANSWER AND MEMORY

63. What do the commandments 1-4 tell us?
How to love God. (Exodus 20:3-11)
64. What do the commandments 5-10 tell us?
How to love other people. (Exodus 20:12-17)

193. God is Watching

He who keeps you will not slumber. Behold, He, who keeps Israel, shall neither slumber nor sleep. (Psalm 121:3-4 NKJV)

God is always watching over us. We can rest and sleep in peace because God is our guard.

~~~~~~

MEMORY VERSE 28
Nor is there salvation in any other, for there is none other name under heaven given among men by which we must be saved (Acts 4:12 NKJV). Salvation comes only through Jesus. No other person can do what he did.

GOD BLESSES AND GUIDES

194. Seek God Early

Those who seek me diligently will find me. (Proverbs 8:17 NKJV)

Seek Jesus Christ early in life. God promises that if you seek him diligently you will find him. It is never too soon to seek the Lord.

195. Love God

Delight yourself also in the LORD, and He shall give you the desires of your heart. (Psalm 37:4 NKJV)

Love God and think about him, then the desire of our heart will be to know him more. God has promised this. True satisfaction is found in God alone.

196. Strength

The LORD will give strength to His people. (Psalm 29:11 NKJV)

The mighty Lord Jesus promises strength to his people when they feel weak; and peace when they are troubled.

197. Righteousness

But seek first the kingdom of God and His righteousness, and all these things shall be added to you. (Matthew 6:33 NKJV)

Be right with God and trust Jesus alone for salvation. God knows what we need. He will take care of us.

198. Blesses

Then the LORD your God will bless you in all that you do. (Deuteronomy 15:18 NKJV)

God promised this to those who were generous and fair. He has promised special care and love to them. The blessing of God is the best gift we can receive.

199. Goodness

Surely goodness and mercy shall follow me all the days of my life. (Psalm 23:6 NKJV)

God's goodness gives us all we need. His mercy blots out our sin because Jesus suffered and died for us on the cross. God promises his goodness to his people for all their life.

200. Directs

Trust in the LORD with all your heart, and lean not on your own understanding. In all your ways acknowledge Him and He shall direct your paths. (Proverbs 3:5-6 NKJV)

God will guide us if we trust him and ask him for help. We should use his Word to show us the right way to live.

QUESTION, ANSWER AND MEMORY

65. What is the summary of the Ten Commandments?
To love the LORD our God with all our heart, and soul and mind, and to love our neighbour as we love ourselves. (Matthew 22:37-40)
66. Who is our neighbour?
Every human being. (Luke 10:36)

201. Guide

For this is God, our God, forever and ever. He will be our guide even to death. (Psalm 48:14 NKJV)

We need a guide all through life, when we are young and when we are old. God is the same today and always. With God and his Word as our guide, we will be safe in this life and forever.

202. Holy Spirit

When He, the Spirit of truth, has come, He will guide you into all truth. (John 16:13 NKJV)

God the Holy Spirit has promised to guide us as we read God's Word and think about it. God's Word is truth and we will not understand it properly without his help and guidance.

~~~~~~~~~~~~~~~~~~~~~~~~~~~~~~~~

QUESTION, ANSWER AND MEMORY

MEMORY VERSE 29

Look to me, and be saved, all you ends of the earth! For I am God, and there is no other (Isaiah 45:22 NKJV). Jesus came to save people from every continent – people of all races and colours and languages. His followers are told to spread the good news to every part of the world.

203. God With Us

My presence will go with you, and I will give you rest (Exodus 33:14 NKJV)

God does not just give instructions to guide us. He actually comes with us to guide us as we go. If he is with us, we will have rest.

GOD'S WORD

204. Eternal

Heaven and earth will pass away, but my words will never pass away. (Mark 13:31 NIV)

God's Word is inspired and enduring. The world will come to an end one day. God promises that his Word will last forever.

205. Prospers

My word … shall not return to me empty, but it shall accomplish that which I purpose, and shall succeed in the thing for which I sent it. (Isaiah 55:11)

God's Word works. He has promised that it will always do what he intends it to do. God uses his Word to bring people to himself and to help them to grow in grace and in knowledge of Jesus Christ.

206. Unchanging

The grass withers, the flower fades, but the word of our God will stand forever. (1 Peter 1:24-25; Isaiah 40:8)

All human beings and human wisdom will pass away like withering flowers. God's Word will never pass away. It is unchanging, always true.

207. Paid the Price

He who hears My word and believes in Him who sent me, has everlasting life and shall not come into judgment. But has passed from death into life. (John 5:24 NKJV)

When we hear God's Word to us in the Bible, we must believe it and trust in God who sent Jesus to die for us. The promise of God is then everlasting life. We will not be punished for our sins because Christ has paid the price.

NOTE FROM THE AUTHOR

God never breaks his promises. Every word he says is true. These promises are for you so it is important that you read and understand them. We all need to learn from God's Word and memorising Scripture as part of your daily routine is one way to do this. However, understanding God's Word is important too. I hope you find the explanations alongside the Scripture verses in this book helpful. Ask God to teach you and your family as you read this book together.

CARINE MACKENZIE

QUESTION, ANSWER AND MEMORY

67. What is the first commandment?
The first commandment is, 'You shall have no other gods before me.' (Exodus 20:3 NKJV)
68. What does the first commandment teach us?
To worship God only. (1 Chronicles 28:9)

MEMORY VERSE 30
Do not be afraid; only believe (Mark 5:36 NKJV). Jesus spoke these comforting words to Jairus when news came that his little girl had just died. Jesus went to the house and restored the little girl to life. Everyone who saw it was amazed.

208. Come to Him

All that the Father gives Me will come to Me, and the one who comes to Me I will by no means cast out. (John 6:37 NKJV)

No one who comes to Christ will be cast away. Even with all our faults and sins and weakness, God will not refuse those who trust in his Son. Those who come to Jesus, have been given to him by God the Father.

209. Eternal Life

For God so loved the world that He gave his only begotten Son, that whoever believes in Him should not perish but have everlasting life. (John 3:16 NKJV)

God's love is so big we cannot measure it. He gave the most wonderful gift, Jesus Christ, his Son. God promised that if we believe in his Son we will not perish but will have eternal life.

210. A Free Gift

The wages of sin is death, but the gift of God is eternal life in Christ Jesus our Lord. (Romans 6:23 NKJV)

Our sin deserves the punishment of death, but through Jesus Christ, God has promised the free gift of eternal life to those who believe and trust him.

211. Good News

Believe on the Lord Jesus Christ and you will be saved, you and your household. (Acts 16:31 NKJV)

This was the gospel message for the Philippian jailer. He was told to trust the Lord Jesus as his Saviour. The good news of the gospel was also for his whole family. If they believed in the Lord Jesus Christ, they too would be saved.

ETERNITY

212. The Last Day

And this is the promise that He has promised us — eternal life. (1 John 2:25 NKJV)

When our bodies die — that is not the end of life. The souls of believers are made perfect and immediately pass into heaven. Our bodies rest in the grave until they are raised again at the last day. God promises his people life that shall never end. Those who are not God's people, will suffer in hell — an awful place prepared for the devil and his angels.

213. Jesus is Alive

Because I live, you will live also. (John 14:19 NKJV)

We have the promise and the hope of eternal life, because Jesus rose again from the dead and is alive now.

214. Perfect Love

Having loved his own which were in the world, he loved them unto the end. (John 13:1 KJV)

God's love reaches everywhere. It is perfect and full. He loves his own all through their lives, right to death and beyond.

QUESTION, ANSWER AND MEMORY

69. What is the second commandment?

The second commandment is, You shall not make for yourself an idol in the form of anything in heaven above or on the earth beneath or in the waters below. You shall not bow down to them or worship them; for I the LORD your God am a jealous God, punishing the children for the sin of the fathers to the third and fourth generation of those who hate me, but showing love to a thousand generations of those who love me and keep my commandments. (Exodus 20:4-6 NIV)

MEMORY VERSE 31

Yet I will rejoice in the LORD, I will joy in the God of my salvation (Habakkuk 3:18 NKJV). When God gives his gift of salvation, it causes great joy in our hearts. This joy comes only from God.

215. Calvary

And if I go and prepare a place for you, I will come again and receive you to Myself, that where I am there you may be also. (John 14:3 NKJV)

Jesus went to the cross at Calvary to prepare a place in heaven for each one of his people. He will come to the earth once more to take his people to heaven with himself.

216. Heaven at Last

You will guide me with Your counsel and afterwards receive me to glory. (Psalm 73:24 NKJV)

God's wise counsel guides us through life. At the end of life, we don't need to be frightened. God has promised to receive us in heaven and welcome us to glory.

217. Completely Safe

I give them eternal life, and they shall never perish, neither shall anyone snatch them out of My hand. (John 10:28 NKJV)

Those who love Jesus are completely safe with him. Nothing can snatch them away from his care. Jesus has all power to keep them secure.

218. God Listens

My God will hear me. (Micah 7:7 NKJV)

If we can truly say that God is 'my God' then we can confidently say that he will hear us. He has promised to listen to those whom he loves.

~~~~~~

THINGS TO DO – PRAY!

Here's another way to remind you about what to pray for. When you bake a cake or cook a recipe there is a short way to write the measurement Teaspoon – it's TSP.

TSP is a good way to remind you of things you ought to do when praying

　　T – Thanks
　　S – Sorry
　　P – Please

This reminds us that it's very important to say 'Thank you' to God first and then to say 'Sorry' before we start asking for the things we want. Sometimes we forget. Sometimes we may think our requests are more important than worshipping and exalting God.

219. God Answers

When you pray, go into your room, and when you have shut your door, pray to your Father who is in the secret place; and your Father who sees in secret will reward you openly. (Matthew 6:6 NKJV)

It is good to pray in private without boasting about it. God hears our secret prayers and promises to answer them openly.

220. Ask God

Ask, and it will be given to you, seek, and you will find; knock, and it will be opened to you. (Matthew 7:7 NKJV)

God has the answer for everything. It is a great privilege to ask him for our needs, to seek his love and to knock for access to his presence.

221. In Jesus' Name

If you ask anything in My name, I will do it. (John 14:14 NKJV)

To pray in the name of Jesus, is to pray in a way that pleases and honours him. It is not a selfish prayer. It is a prayer for the glory of Jesus, and for his kingdom. It is not just adding 'for Jesus' sake' at the end of our prayer.

~~~~~~~~~~~~~~~~~~~~

QUESTION, ANSWER AND MEMORY

70. What does the second commandment tell us to do?
To worship God in the way that he tells us in his Word, and not to use man-made idols or statues. (Deuteronomy 12:32)

222. God Provides

Before they call, I will answer. (Isaiah 65:24 NKJV)

God knows us better than we know ourselves. Sometimes the answer to our prayer is on the way, before we even pray. God provides for every need.

223. Wisdom

If any of you lacks wisdom, let him ask of God, who gives to all liberally and without reproach, and it will be given to him. (James 1:5 NKJV)

We all lack wisdom and need God's help for every day. God has promised wisdom to those who ask him in faith.

MEMORY VERSE 32
Believe on the Lord Jesus Christ, and you will be saved, you and your household (Acts 16:31 NKJV). This was the answer Paul and Silas gave when a man asked 'What must I do to be saved?' The important message for him and for his family was to BELIEVE on the Lord Jesus Christ. This is important for us too.

SIN

224. Resist the Devil

Submit to God. Resist the devil and he will flee from you. Draw near to God and He will draw near to you. (James 4:7-8 NKJV)

If God is our Lord, the devil is defeated. If we resist the devil, he will be forced away, and God will be very near to us.

225. Confess

If we confess our sins, He is faithful and just to forgive us our sins, and to cleanse us from all unrighteousness. (1 John 1:9 NKJV)

Sin leaves a stain on our lives. If we confess our sins to our faithful and just Father God, he will deal with that stain. He will forgive every sin through Jesus Christ.

226. God is Gracious

The LORD is merciful and gracious … He has not dealt with us according to our sins, nor punished us according to our iniquities. (Psalm 103:8, 10 NKJV)

Our sins deserve great punishment. God has graciously accepted the suffering of Jesus Christ in our place. Because he suffered, we go free.

227. Saviour

You shall call his name JESUS, for He will save his people from their sins. (Matthew 1:21 NKJV)

When God the Son came to this world as a baby, Joseph was told by God the Father to give him the name JESUS, which means 'Saviour'. The promise was given that he would save his people from their sins. This is what Jesus has done by dying on the cross and taking the punishment of our sins.

228. Confess and Forsake

He who covers his sins will not prosper, but whoever confesses and forsakes them will have mercy. (Proverbs 28:13 NKJV)

If we try to cover up our sin and pretend we have done nothing wrong, we will be in big trouble. But if we tell God about our sin and turn away from it, God promises to have mercy and forgive.

QUESTION, ANSWER AND MEMORY

71. What is the third commandment?
The third commandment is, 'You shall not misuse the name of the LORD your God, for the LORD will not hold anyone guiltless who misuses his name' (Exodus 20:7 NIV).
72. What does the third commandment tell us to do?
To honour God's name and not to use God's name in a careless way. (Psalm 29:2)

MEMORY VERSE 33
Open my eyes, that I may see wondrous things from your law (Psalm 119:18). Before we read the Bible, it is good to pray like this, asking God to give us the understanding to see the wonderful truths in his word.

229. Forgive and Forget

For I will forgive their iniquity, and I will remember their sin no more.
(Jeremiah 31:34; Hebrews 10:17)

God promises not only to forgive the sin of his people, but to forget it completely. Our sins are blotted out by the blood of Jesus Christ who died on the cross at Calvary. We should trust him and love him, who first loved us.

FEAR

230. Problems

Come to Me, all you who labour and are heavy laden, and I will give you rest. (Matthew 11:28 NKJV)

If we come to Jesus with our problems of sadness, loneliness and anxiety, he has promised to help us and give us peace in our hearts.

231. Don't Be Afraid

Fear not, for I am with you; be not dismayed, for I am your God. I will strengthen you, yes, I will help you, I will uphold you with My righteous right hand. (Isaiah 41:10 NKJV)

God often tells us not to be afraid. He has promised to be with us, to strengthen, help and uphold. With these wonderful promises from the faithful God, we should never be afraid.

232. Don't Be Worried

Be anxious for nothing, but in everything by prayer and supplication, with thanksgiving, let your requests be made to God; and the peace of God which surpasses all understanding will guard your hearts and minds through Christ Jesus. (Philippians 4:6-7 NKJV)

God asks us to pray thankfully to him about everything. He then gives us his peace, which is more wonderful than we can imagine. He does this because of Jesus.

233. We Will Have Problems

Many are the afflictions of the righteous, but the LORD delivers him out of them all. (Psalm 34:19 NKJV)

God does not promise an easy life with no problems. He tells us we will have difficulties. But he will be with us and take us through all our problems.

234. God is Strong

My grace is sufficient for you, for My strength is made perfect in weakness. (2 Corinthians 12:9 NKJV)

When we are weak, God's strength is shown more clearly. He gives us the grace that we need, just when we need it.

235. Tell God All About It

Cast your burden on the LORD and he shall sustain you. (Psalm 55:22 NKJV)

God asks us to tell him all our problems. He wants to carry them for us. If we trust him, he will uphold us in all the struggles of life.

236. God's Promise Never Fails

The LORD, He is the One who goes before you. He will be with you; he will not leave you nor forsake you; do not fear nor be dismayed. (Deuteronomy 31:8 NKJV)

God is with us everywhere. If we travel far away, go to live in a new town, start in a new school — he is there too. His promise never fails.

QUESTION, ANSWER AND MEMORY

73. What is the fourth commandment?

The fourth commandment is, Remember the Sabbath day to keep it holy. Six days you shall labour, and do all your work, but the seventh day is a Sabbath to the LORD your God. On it you shall not do any work, you, or your son, or your daughter, your male servant, or your female servant, or your livestock, or the sojourner who is within your gates. For in six days the LORD made heaven and earth, the sea and all that is in them, and rested on the seventh day. Therefore the LORD blessed the Sabbath day and made it holy. (Exodus 20:8-11)

MEMORY VERSE 34

Let us therefore come boldly to the throne of grace, that we may obtain mercy and find grace to help in time of need (Hebrews 4:16 NKJV). We should not be afraid to pray. Our loving, merciful God wants us to come to him. He gives mercy and forgiveness to the repentant sinner and love and grace to the needy person.

237. Faithful and True

The LORD is faithful in all his words and kind in all his works
(Psalm 145:13)

God's Word is faithful and true. He has made many promises to his people, which we are to believe. The promises will encourage us when we are afraid, or troubled by sin. His promises help us to pray and guide us through life. They remind us of his care and love to us, of his many blessings and the promise of salvation through Jesus Christ.

All of us have to face death, and eternity beyond that. Our sin deserves God's anger and punishment, but Jesus suffered and died on the cross to pay the price for the sins of his people. Jesus Christ has promised to save all who believe in him.

Let's Think About

THE BIBLE

238. God Wrote It

All Scripture is breathed out by God.
(2 Timothy 3:16)

God has given us a wonderful gift, the Bible. This is an amazing book, written by about forty different people, each one inspired by God, the Holy Spirit. So it is one complete book – God is the author.

The Bible is also known as the Scriptures, which means writings. God's Word has been written down and preserved through the centuries. Some was written in Hebrew and some in Greek, but it has been translated into many languages and we have it now in our own language.

239. The Old Testament

And beginning with Moses and all the Prophets, he (Jesus) interpreted to them in all the Scriptures the things concerning himself. (Luke 24:27)

The Bible is divided into two sections, called the Old Testament and the New Testament. The Old Testament has thirty-nine books originally written in the Hebrew language.

Jesus knew these Scriptures very well and quoted from them. He fulfilled the prophecy about himself in his life and death and resurrection. The Old Testament points to the Lord Jesus – the Son of God who came to earth as a human with the purpose of saving his people from their sins.

240. New Testament

… it seemed good to me also, having followed all things closely for some time past, to write an orderly account for you, most excellent Theophilus, that you may have certainty concerning the things you have been taught. (Luke 1:3-4)

The New Testament has twenty-seven books originally written in Greek. The Gospels tell about Jesus' life and ministry. Acts records the beginning of the Christian church. The Epistles are the teaching of the apostles to the early church. Revelation is a prophetic book, revealing future events.

Each book is now divided into chapters. Each chapter is divided into verses. This makes it easier for us to find a particular sentence in the book.

WHAT IS THE WORD OF GOD?

241. The Word of God is True

Your word is truth. (John 17:17)
And now, O Lord God, you are God, and your words are true. (2 Samuel 7:28)
Every word of God proves true. (Proverbs 30:5)

God is a God of truth. He does not lie, or exaggerate or try to deceive anyone. His Word, the Bible, is completely true. In court, a witness promises to tell the truth, the whole truth and nothing but the truth. God is the most faithful witness. The Lord Jesus told us that one of his names is 'The Truth' (John 14:6). We can trust him completely.

242. The Word of God Lasts Forever

Heaven and earth will pass away, but my words will not pass away. (Mark 13:31)
The grass withers, the flower fades, but the word of our God will stand forever. (Isaiah 40:8)

The clothes you have today will one day wear out. Your toys will break and be thrown away. The flowers in the garden wither and die. God tells us that even the world we live in, will be burned up and come to an end. But God's Word will never be destroyed. It will last forever.

QUESTION, ANSWER AND MEMORY

74. What does the fourth commandment tell us?
To keep the Sabbath holy. (Leviticus 19:30)
75. What day of the week is the Christian Sabbath?
The first day of the week or Lord's Day on which Christ rose from the dead. (Acts 20:7. Revelation 1:10)

MEMORY VERSE 35
In everything give thanks; for this is the will of God in Christ Jesus for you (1 Thessalonians 5:18 NKJV). Prayer is not just asking for God to supply our needs and sort out our problems. An important part of prayer is saying 'Thank you' for everything.

NOTE FROM THE AUTHOR

The Bible tells us that we should train up a child in the way he should go; and when he is old, he will not depart from it (Proverbs 22:6).

Children need to know about God and his Word. We all do. What do we need to know? We need to know that God's Word is true, eternal, pure, living, perfect, inspired and without error.

It is exciting to see God's Word at work in our world. When you are worshipping God and studying his Word make sure you take time to pray and to find out about specific points to pray for. Books like *40 Days 40 Bites* by Trudi Parkes are excellent resources for this.

243. Pure

The words of the LORD are pure words, like silver refined in a furnace. (Psalm 12:6)

After silver is mined from the ground, it is melted and heated to a very high temperature. The impurities rise to the surface and the silversmith scoops them off. Eventually the silver is pure and shining.

God's Word is like that pure silver. No impurities spoil the perfection. We are sinners; our lives are not pure. Jesus shed his blood on the cross and his blood cleanses us from all sin.

244. Living and Active

For the word of God is living and active, sharper than any two-edged sword ... discerning the thoughts and intentions of the heart. (Hebrews 4:12)

God's Word is not merely a collection of stories and interesting facts. God's Word works. It reaches into a person's mind and heart and convinces of sin. It persuades us that the only way to be truly happy is to trust in the Lord Jesus, who died on the cross to forgive our sins.

It prods our conscience to correct us when we do wrong. It helps us to praise and thank God for his grace and love and mercy.

245. Perfect

The law of the LORD is perfect, reviving the soul. (Psalm 19:7)

We are all born as sinners, natural enemies of God. To be right with God, our lives have to be turned around from loving sin to trusting in the Lord Jesus Christ. This is called conversion. God's Holy Spirit works in the heart and soul. God's Word is the ideal, perfect means to bring about this change.

246. Inspired

All Scripture is breathed out by God and profitable for teaching, for reproof, for correction, and for training in righteousness. (2 Timothy 3:16)

The Bible writers, like Matthew, Paul and Isaiah wrote their books not because they thought it would be a good idea. They were moved by the Holy Spirit to speak from God. God inspired the Bible writers. He breathed out his thoughts and words into their minds and they wrote it down. This makes the Bible a unique book.

247. No Errors

Every word of God proves true; he is a shield to those who take refuge in him. (Proverbs 30:5)

The Bible is completely true and without error in any part. Someone who copied or translated the manuscript could make a mistake, but the original, as God first gave it, is always correct. To disbelieve the Bible is to disbelieve God. God cannot lie. His Word, the Bible, does not lie either.

Two big words describe this –

The Bible is infallible – always right and true.

The Bible is inerrant – never makes a mistake.

We can completely trust God and his Word.

248. The Lord Jesus

The name by which he is called is The Word of God. (Revelation 19:13) In the beginning was the Word, and the Word was with God, and the Word was God. (John 1:1)

The Word of God is one of the names given to God the Son, who came to this world to be the Saviour of sinners. He was born in Bethlehem, and given the name Jesus. He lived as a man in our world.

But he never ceased to be God the Son, who has existed from all eternity. This is an amazing truth which should make us want to worship him.

WHAT DOES THE WORD OF GOD DO?

249. It Created Everything

By faith we understand that the universe was created by the word of God. (Hebrews 11:3)

God created the whole world by his powerful Word. God said, 'Let there be light,' and there was light. God said, 'Let the waters under the heavens be gathered into one place, and let the dry land appear.' And it was so.

God said, 'Let the earth sprout vegetation' and it was so. God said, 'Let there be lights in the heavens' and it was so. With a word, God created birds, sea creatures and animals.

QUESTION, ANSWER AND MEMORY

76. What should we do on the Sabbath?
We should worship God with his people and on our own, pray to him, praise him, read or listen to his Word and do good to other people (Isaiah 58:13-14).
77. What is the fifth commandment?
The fifth commandment is, Honour your father and mother, that your days may be long in the land that the LORD your God is giving you (Exodus 20:12).

MEMORY VERSE 36
Ask, and it will be given to you; seek, and you will find; knock, and it will be opened to you (Matthew 7:7). Jesus told us to come to God in prayer – to ask and to seek and to knock. God is gracious and will answer our prayers, but not always in the way or at the time that we think best.

250. It Teaches Us About God

You search the Scriptures because you think that in them you have eternal life; and it is they that bear witness about me. (John 5:39)

The Bible teaches us about God. It tells us what he is — holy, powerful, good, just, wise, loving. The Bible teaches us what God has done for us — giving us life, breath, food, shelter, family — and a Saviour, the Lord Jesus, to deal with our sin and grant us forgiveness.

The Old Testament stories and prophecies point to the coming Saviour; the Gospels tell about his life and death; the Epistles tell of how Jesus' life and death make all the difference to us.

251. It Makes Us Wise for Salvation

… and how from childhood you have been acquainted with the sacred writings, which are able to make you wise for salvation through faith in Christ Jesus. (2 Timothy 3:15)

The Lord Jesus came to this world to be the Saviour of sinners. God tells us about his Son, the Saviour, in his Word. We learn about his plan of salvation in the Bible. It speaks God's message to our heart — convincing us of our sin and assuring us of God's grace and mercy. This makes us wise for salvation.

252. It Teaches Us What to Do

Let us hear the conclusion of the whole matter: Fear God, and keep his commandments: for this is the whole duty of man. (Ecclesiastes 12:13 KJV)

The great, holy God, our Creator, requires us to be obedient to him and his law. This is given to us in detail in the Bible. We must honour and respect God and live in a way that is pleasing to him.

Often we fall into sin and wish to please ourselves. God's Word challenges us and calls us back to God. Jesus kept the law perfectly and we must trust in him.

253. It Purifies

How can a young man keep his way pure? By guarding it according to your word. (Psalm 119:9)

If we ignore God's Word, we will soon be taken over by sin. We will think bad thoughts; we will say wrong words — lies and boasting and unkindness; we will do sinful actions. Only the Lord through his word can keep a person, young or old, from falling into the sin that stains our life.

254. It Gives Joy to the Heart

Your words became to me a joy and the delight of my heart. (Jeremiah 15:16)

If we love the Lord, we love to read or listen to his Word. It brings a lasting joy and satisfaction as it tells us about what Jesus Christ has done for us and continues to do for us. This joy makes us want to praise God and thank him for his love and goodness to us.

255. It is Hidden in the Heart

I have stored up your word in my heart, that I might not sin against you. (Psalm 119:11)

It is a good thing to memorise verses from the Bible. When we are tempted to sin, God's Word will strengthen us and keep us from telling a lie or stealing or any of the sins that can bother us. If we know some verses off by heart we can think about them as we lie in bed in the dark. God the Holy Spirit brings to our minds the Word that we have learned.

256. The Word of God is Like a Seed

Now the parable is this: 'The seed is the word of God.' (Luke 8:11)

Jesus told a story comparing the Word of God to seeds. When the farmer sowed the seed it fell on different types of ground. Some withered and died, but some multiplied and grew and produced more grain. When you hear the Word of God, does it flourish and produce in your heart the fruit of the Spirit like love, joy, and peace? If we ignore the Word of God or think that other things are more important, then we do not produce good fruit in our lives.

QUESTION, ANSWER AND MEMORY

78. What does the fifth commandment tell us to do?
To love and obey our parents and all people in authority over us (Colossians 3:20)
79. What is the sixth commandment?
The sixth commandment is, You shall not murder. (Exodus 20:13)

MEMORY VERSE 37
Be anxious for nothing, but in everything by prayer and supplication, with thanksgiving, let your requests be made known to God (Philippians 4:6 NKJV). No worry is too big to take to God. No worry is too small to take to God. We should tell him about everything remembering to be thankful for all his goodness.

257. It is like a Sword

Take the helmet of salvation, and the sword of the Spirit, which is the word of God. (Ephesians 6:17 NKJV)

A soldier has to be armed. Long ago he would use a sword to fight the enemy. The Christian has an enemy too – the devil. We must always be ready to use our sword, the Word of God, to fight against the devil. Jesus used the Word of God to defeat the devil who was tempting him to sin. Three times he said, 'It is written …' and quoted a verse from the book of Deuteronomy (See Luke chapter 4:1-13).

258. It is Like a Fire

'Is not my word like fire?' declares the LORD. (Jeremiah 23:29)

A fire can sweep through a forest or a building, destroying everything in its path. God's Word is as powerful as a fire. It pronounces judgement on people who hate God or ignore God and his law. God's judgement is perfect and just and certain for those who refuse God and his Word. Jesus Christ has taken the punishment for the sin of those who trust in him.

259. It is Like Food

I have not departed from the commandment of his lips; I have treasured the words of his mouth more than my portion of food. (Job 23:12)

Job, who lived many years ago, had lots of problems. His family were killed, his possessions destroyed; his body covered with horrible boils. His wife was no help, nor were his friends. But Job could say that he loved God's words more than his necessary food.

Without food we could not live. The Bible, God's Word, gives nourishment and life to our souls. Food in the fridge does not nourish our body. We have to eat it to get any benefit. The Bible sitting on the shelf does us no good. We have to read it or listen to it to see an effect in our daily lives.

260. It is Like a Hammer

Is not My word … like a hammer that breaks the rock in pieces? (Jeremiah 23:29 NKJV)

The pounding of a sledge hammer can break strong rock in pieces. The truth of God's Word is strong and can break the hardest heart and change the sinner. When God converts the sinner, he gives him a new heart to love and trust him.

God's Word cannot be broken – even when evil people misuse it or tell lies about it – God's Word, like a hammer, will destroy that falsehood.

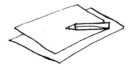

261. It is Like a Lamp

Your word is a lamp to my feet and a light to my path. (Psalm 119:105 NKJV)

If you go out walking on a dark night, it is wise to take a torch with you. The bright light dispels the darkness and helps you on your way. In the dark we are more likely to stumble and fall.

God's Word is like a lamp, guiding us on the right way and keeping us from falling into temptation and sin. The words of the Bible dispel the darkness of sin and guide us on our journey through life.

262. It is Like Milk

Like newborn infants, long for the pure spiritual milk, that by it you may grow up into salvation. (1 Peter 2:2)

When a baby cries, it is often because he is hungry and is longing for some milk. When he gets it, he is happy. It is the regular feeding with milk that makes him grow.

Regularly reading or hearing God's Word helps us to grow in grace and in the knowledge of God. If we are starved of God's Word, our spiritual life will suffer and make us unhappy. But God's Word will satisfy our souls and do us good.

263. It is Like Solid Food

Everyone who lives on milk is unskilled in the word of righteousness, since he is a child. But solid food is for the mature. (Hebrews 5:13-14)

Babies drink milk, but as we grow up, we move on to solid food, like meat and vegetables. When we are young, we learn about God's Word – starting with the simple things. As we grow older, we will want to learn more and more. Even the oldest, most clever person will always find something to learn in God's Word.

~~~~~~~~~~

QUESTION, ANSWER AND MEMORY

80. What does the sixth commandment tell us to do?
Not to take the life of another or to fight with anyone. (Psalm 82:3-4. Matthew 5:21-22).
81. What is the seventh commandment?
The seventh commandment is, 'You shall not commit adultery.' (Exodus 20:14)

MEMORY VERSE 38
Rejoice in the Lord always; again I will say, rejoice. (Philippians 4:4)
When we remember what God has done for us and is still doing for us everyday, we have good reason to be joyful.

264. It is More Precious than Gold

(The words of the Lord are) more to be desired than gold, even much fine gold. (Psalm 19:10)

Gold is a precious and beautiful metal which is made into coins, jewellery and other lovely things. A rich man will own lots of precious gold items. The Word of God is even more valuable. God has given us this amazing gift and we should value it more than any gold object we possess.

265. It is Sweeter than Honey

(The words of God are) sweeter also than honey and drippings of the honeycomb. (Psalm 19:10)

Honey, made by the bees, is delicious and so sweet. It is nourishing and sustaining and very pleasant to taste. God's Word is so good to read and to think about. It gives us strength for our daily life, comfort in sadness and satisfies all our needs.

266. God's Word in Your Language

How precious to me are your thoughts, O God! How vast is the sum of them! (Psalm 139:17)

God has graciously given us his Word, which has been preserved by him through the ages and translated into a language that we can understand. What a precious gift!

In it God tells us all that we need to believe about him. It tells us the gospel of the Lord Jesus Christ who is the only way of salvation from sin, leading to eternal life.

267. God's Word Teaches You

Give ear, O my people, to my teaching; incline your ears to the words of my mouth! (Psalm 78:1)

God's Word teaches us what kind of behaviour God asks of us, in order to serve and glorify him. Pray that all that you have learned will cause you to see just how valuable the Bible is. May the Word of God that you have read help you to praise and thank God for his kindness and love.

Let's Think About

BIBLE

PRAYERS

PHILIP ROSS

268. Teaching the Scriptures

I am reminded of your sincere faith, a faith that dwelt first in your grandmother Lois and your mother Eunice and now, I am sure, dwells in you as well. (2 Timothy 1:5)

Thousands of years ago, Moses told parents to teach God's words to their children. Eunice was a lady who remembered Moses' instructions. She taught Timothy, her son, so that when he grew up he was able to teach others. His friend, Paul, reminded him that he had known the Bible since he was little. Timothy might not have understood everything when he was young, but the Scriptures made him wise. When he was older, he even went to prison because of his sincere faith in Jesus.

269. Learn to Pray

Now Jesus was praying in a certain place, and when he finished, one of his disciples said to him, 'Lord, teach us to pray, as John taught his disciples.' (Luke 11:1)

One thing that Timothy learned from the Bible was how to pray. He heard how believers spoke to God and what they asked for. You too need to learn how to pray. Not one of us knows how to pray as we should, but the Bible teaches us and gives us many examples.

Perhaps you already know the Lord's Prayer, which Jesus taught his disciples. There are more prayers for you to learn, based on different parts of the Bible. Make them your own. God promises to answer.

NOTE FROM THE AUTHOR

Most of the prayers in this next part of the book are short and will not be too hard to remember. Some are a little longer and will need a bit more effort. Below every prayer are a few sentences, to help you understand what it is about. If you want to learn more, you can look up the part of the Bible where the words come from. Sometimes, you will need someone to explain things to you.

You will learn different names and titles for God. You will worship him as your Creator, Saviour, and King. You will admit your badness and sin. You will ask for everything that you need to make you good and bring you to heaven.

Remember that Jesus said, 'If you ask for anything in my name, I will do it.'

Philip Ross

270. Jesus Will Never Go Away

(Acts 7:59; Revelation 1:17; Psalm 102:25; Hebrews 1:10-11)

Lord Jesus, the First and the Last,
in the beginning
you laid the foundations
of the earth,
and the heavens
are the work of your hands.
They will perish,
but you will remain.

Some day God will destroy the whole world. Nothing will be left. Even Mount Everest will melt away like wax on a candle. But the Lord Jesus will never go away. He was here before Mount Everest. He made everything. And when everything has gone, he will still be here. You can only be safe with him.

~~~~~~~~~~

QUESTION, ANSWER AND MEMORY

82. What does the seventh commandment tell us to do?
To be pure in our thoughts, words and behaviour. (2 Timothy 2:22)
83. What is the eighth commandment?
The eighth commandment is, 'You shall not steal.' (Exodus 20:15)

MEMORY VERSE 39
Seek the Lord while he may be found, call upon him while he is near. (Isaiah 55:6). God invites us to seek him and to pray to him for salvation. We should not put this off until a later date as that may be too late. The best time is NOW.

271. Count Your Days

(James 4:14; Psalm 90:2, 12)

Everlasting God,
my life is like a mist
that appears for a little while
and then it is gone;
teach me to count my days
so that I will gain a wise heart.

Go outside on a frosty morning and you will see your breath. But pay attention! As soon as it leaves your mouth, it will disappear. You cannot get it back. Your life is like that. Is it hard to understand that your life is so short? Then ask God to teach you and make you wise.

272. My Refuge

(Psalm 46:7; Genesis 28:20)

God of Jacob, my refuge,
be with me and keep me
in the way that I go.
Give me bread to eat
and clothes to wear.

One night God spoke to Jacob. 'I am with you', he said. 'I will watch over you wherever you go.' Jacob believed God. God took care of him. Do you ask God to look after you? If you believe his promises, he will always provide for you.

273. Born in Iniquity

(Psalm 51:5)

Behold, I was born in iniquity,
and in sin
my mother conceived me.

Do you ever wonder, 'Why do I keep doing bad things?' Perhaps you think, 'The problem is, I am bad.' Yes, you are. But, you need to tell God all about it. Admit that you were never good. Not even when you were tiny. He knows when we only pretend to be good.

274. Merciful

(Psalm 51:17; Luke 18:13)

O God, you will not despise
a broken and a contrite heart.
Be merciful to me a sinner.

You know that God hates you doing wrong. But do you hate it? Do you feel sad to have offended God? Then you should tell him. God will always love you if you cry in your heart about your sin. And when you ask him to forgive you, he will be very kind.

275. A Seed

(Luke 8:15)

Give me an honest
and good heart,
so that when I hear your word,
I will remember it
and bear fruit.

God's Word is like seed. It can only grow in good ground. The trouble is that our hearts are like bad ground. But if God gives you a good heart, you will hear and remember his Word. You will keep it in mind and always produce good fruit.

276. Faithful

(1 Corinthians 1:9)

Faithful God,
call me into the fellowship
of your Son,
Jesus Christ our Lord.

Perhaps someone once asked you, 'Will you be my friend?' but you did not listen. Or, you said, 'Yes, I will be your friend,' but you soon forgot one another. It is different with God. Even if you are far away, you will hear when he calls you to be close to his Son. He will always keep you in his family.

277. Joy that Lasts

(Psalm 73:25)

Whom have I in heaven but you?
And there is nothing on earth
that I desire besides you.

Have you noticed that very bad people often have good things and not much trouble? If God is your guide, you know that these people will not live happily forever. You see that only God can give you joy that lasts. Do you want him more than anything else?

QUESTION, ANSWER AND MEMORY

84. What does the eighth commandment tell us to do?
To be honest and to work hard to look after ourselves and others, and to respect the property of others. (Romans 12:17)
85. What is the ninth commandment?
The ninth commandment is, 'You shall not bear false witness against your neighbour.' (Exodus 20:16)
86. What does the ninth commandment tell us to do?
To tell the truth at all times. (Zechariah 8:16)

MEMORY VERSE 40
Remember also your Creator in the days of your youth (Ecclesiastes 12:1). Boys and girls are asked by God to remember him when they are young. We have to remember that God is our Creator. He made us and everything in the world.

278. Call on the Lord

(Psalm 116:1)

I love you LORD,
because you have heard my voice
and my cries for mercy.

Lots of people cry to the LORD when
they are in trouble. But when their problems go away they
forget about him. Do not be like that. Call on the LORD for as
long as you live. And when he helps you, say,

'I love you LORD.'

279. God Protects

(Psalm 84)

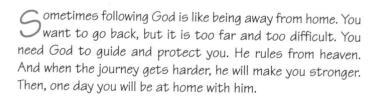

O LORD of hosts,
our sun and shield;
give me grace and glory
to go on from strength to strength
until I appear before you
in your dwelling-place.

Sometimes following God is like being away from home. You
want to go back, but it is too far and too difficult. You
need God to guide and protect you. He rules from heaven.
And when the journey gets harder, he will make you stronger.
Then, one day you will be at home with him.

280. No One Greater

(1 Corinthians 2:8; Psalm 72:19)

Lord of Glory,
let your glorious name
be blessed forever.
Let the whole earth
be filled with your glory.

Jesus is not like other kings. Most people do not see how great he is. Has God shown you Jesus? Then you will never see anyone greater. You want everyone to realize that no one is more wonderful. You want the whole world to see Jesus' glory.

281. The Rock

(Deuteronomy 32:4)

LORD, you are the Rock,
your work is perfect,
all your ways are justice.
You are a God of faithfulness
and without iniquity,
you are just and upright.

Do you trust everyone? Probably not. Some people are mean and twisted. There is one person who can always be trusted: the LORD. He is always honest, fair, and reliable. He is absolutely perfect. If you want to be safe, stay close to him.

282. God is King

(Isaiah 33:22)

LORD, you are our judge,
our lawgiver,
and our king.
Save us.

Christian people cannot do anything without Jesus. No one else is wise enough to guide us. Whenever we make our own rules, we end up in a big mess. The men who lead us die or fail. But the LORD reigns forever. He is the only one who can save his people.

283. Mercy and Forgiveness

(Daniel 9:8-9)

O Lord our God,
to us belongs open shame
because we have
sinned against you,
but to you belong
mercy and forgiveness.

Daniel was a good man. He loved God's people. They were suffering because they turned away from God. Can you imagine how sad that made Daniel? He felt ashamed. But he spoke to God about all their failures.

Daniel understood that although God corrects his children, he never leaves them.

284. The God of Truth

(Psalm 31:5; 1 John 1:8)

O Lord, the God of truth,
if I say that I have no sin,
I deceive myself,
and the truth is not in me.

If you have black hair, but you say, 'I am sure my hair is red,' you will not trick anyone. Everyone sees your black hair. In the same way, you cannot make God think that you do nothing wrong. He sees everything. Admit the truth about yourself.

QUESTION, ANSWER AND MEMORY

87. What is the tenth commandment?
The tenth commandment is, 'You shall not covet your neighbour's house. You shall not covet your neighbour's wife, or his male servant or his female servant, or his ox, or donkey, or anything that is your neighbour's.' (Exodus 20:17)
88. What does the tenth commandment tell us to do?
To be content with what we have and not to be envious of others (1 Timothy 6:8).

MEMORY VERSE 41
You shall love the Lord your God with all your heart, with all your soul, and with all your strength (Deuteronomy 6:5 NKJV). The Lord God requires our complete love – we ought to love him most of all – with all of our heart, soul and strength.

285. Ask God for Help

(1 Peter 1:3; John 6:44)

God and Father
of our Lord Jesus Christ,
draw me to your Son
or else I will be
unable to come to him.

Suppose you offered something good to someone, but they would not take it. Jesus said that we are all like that with him. He offers himself, but you cannot come to Jesus unless God the Father gives you the power. That is why you need to ask for his help.

286. The Perfect Shepherd

(John 10:11; Isaiah 40:11)

Good Shepherd, feed me,
gather me like a lamb in your arms,
and carry me in your bosom.

Long ago God chose kings and leaders to be like good shepherds. But often they took care of themselves and not God's people. Then God promised that he would come to look after them himself. And he did. Our Lord Jesus is the perfect shepherd. You can trust him to look after you. He even gave his life for the sheep.

287. Peace and Hope and Joy

(Romans 15:13)

God of hope,
fill me with joy
and peace
in believing.

Are you only happy when good things are happening? Not if you trust in God. Then you can be glad even when life is hard. You believe his wonderful promises for the future, so you do not need to worry. And no matter what happens, God fills you with joy.

288. Poverty or Riches?

(Proverbs 30:8)

Give me neither poverty
nor riches;
feed me with the food
that I need.

People think that money makes you happy. Hardly anyone wants to be poor. But it is good to be neither rich nor poor. Being rich is dangerous. You might forget that you need God. That does not mean it is good to be poor. Then you might steal. It is best to have just what you need.

289. Comfort and Mercies

(2 Corinthians 1:3; 1 Corinthians 1:8)

God of all comfort,
Father of mercies,
strengthen me to the end,
so that I will be blameless
on the day
of our Lord Jesus Christ.

One day the Lord Jesus will return to judge everyone. Will you be perfect when he comes? Only if you understand that you are weak. Then you will ask God for strength to do what is right. He is a sympathetic Father who always encourages his children.

290. Slow to Anger

(Exodus 34:6-8)

I bow before you, the LORD, the LORD, a God merciful and gracious, slow to anger, and abounding in loving-kindness and truth. You keep loving-kindness for thousands, forgiving iniquity and transgression and sin. But you will by no means clear the guilty, visiting the iniquity of the fathers on the children and the children's children, to the third and fourth generation.

What kind of person is God? He is greater than you can imagine. When his children go astray, he still loves them. He forgives all kinds of evil. Think of how kind he is. But remember that he never ignores our guilt. What you do matters. It affects you and others.

291. The Hairs on Your Head

(Psalm 40:12-13)

My iniquities are more than
the hairs of my head;
my heart fails me.
Be pleased, O LORD,
to deliver me! O LORD,
come quickly to help me!

It is difficult to count the hairs on your head. It is even harder to count your sins. They are more than the hairs on your head. And they cause you such trouble. Have you discovered that? Then you know that the LORD needs to take away your sin. Who else can rescue you?

292. God is Good

(1 Peter 2:1-3; Psalm 34:8)

Like a newborn baby,
may I long for
the pure milk of the word.
Then I will taste
and see that you are good.

Tiny babies love to drink milk. Are you like that with the Bible? God's Word will make you grow and keep you right. As you believe his promises, you will discover that he is good. The LORD will rescue you from trouble. He will make sure that you have whatever is good for you.

293. Father God

(Romans 8:15; Psalm 89:26-27)

Give me your Spirit
so that I will cry,
'You are my Father, my God,
and the Rock of my salvation.'

God keeps his children safe. He is like a rock. Nothing blows him around. But he is not hard and cold. Jesus called him 'Father'. Do you? If you ask him, God will give you his Spirit. King Jesus, his firstborn, will be your brother. And you too will call God 'Father'.

QUESTION, ANSWER AND MEMORY

89. Can we obey the Ten Commandments perfectly?
No. We break them every day in thought, word and deed. (Psalm 14:3)
90. Has anyone ever perfectly obeyed the Ten Commandments?
Only the Lord Jesus Christ, who is God and man in one person, has perfectly obeyed the Ten Commandments. (Hebrews 4:15, 1 Peter 2:22)

MEMORY VERSE 42
Be strong and of good courage; do not be afraid, nor be dismayed, for the LORD your God is with you wherever you go (Joshua 1:9). God spoke these words to Joshua. We can believe them too. If God is with us, we need never be afraid.

294. Be Different

(Philippians 2:14-15)

Teach me to do everything
without grumbling or arguing
so that I may be blameless
and innocent – shining
like a light in the world.

It is easy to complain and argue. Everyone does. But you should be different. You must be pure like Jesus. He was not selfish. When he was badly treated, he did not grumble. If you are like him, you will shine like a bright star in the night sky.

295. Resist the Devil

(Nehemiah 1:4; James 4:7)

God of heaven,
help me to submit to you
and resist the devil
so that he will flee from me.

The devil is powerful. He works hard to make you disobey God. But he is also a coward. He knows that you will fight against him when he sees that you serve God. And when you do that, Satan will run away. The devil always loses when the God of heaven is on your side.

296. Love God

(Deuteronomy 6:5; Leviticus 19:18; Mark 12:29-31)

O Lord my God,
please help me to love you
with all my heart,
and with all my soul,
and with all my mind.
And help me to love my neighbour
as myself.

God gave his people laws so that they would know how to behave. You can read them in the first books of the Bible. They will teach you that God expects you to love him as completely as he loves his own children. He also wants you to care about others as much as you care about yourself.

297. The Resurrection

(Ephesians 1:17; Philippians 3:10)

God of our Lord Jesus Christ,
Father of glory,
I want to know Christ
and the power of his resurrection.

God raised Jesus from the dead. He is alive. Knowing Jesus is not the same as remembering a dead person. It is like being with someone who is full of life. If you trust in Jesus then nothing is more important to you than knowing him. You want his power to change your life.

298. Shine Like the Sun

(Matthew 13:41 43; 22:32; Daniel 12:2 3)

God of the living,
use me to lead many
to righteousness
so that I will shine
like the sun in your kingdom.

Will it be a good day for you, when God raises the dead? It depends what kind of person you are now. If you do not love God, it will be dreadful. But if you are someone who teaches others to follow him, it will be a wonderful day. God will change you. He will make you splendid forever.

299. God Never Sleeps

(Psalm 121)

LORD, you never slumber or sleep.
Watch over me
when I go out
and when I come in.
Protect me day and night,
now and for evermore.

Soldiers die, or ships sink, if someone who should be looking out for danger, falls asleep. You cannot trust anyone to stay awake, except the LORD. He never gets sleepy and he sees every danger you will meet. Whatever may happen, he can protect you. Trust no one else with your life.

300. Exalt Your God

(Psalm 118:28-29)

You are my God,
and I will give thanks to you;
you are my God;
I will exalt you.
Give thanks to the LORD
for his loving kindness lasts forever.

The Bible tells how God divided the Red Sea for the Israelites. They walked across on dry land to escape Pharaoh. Even more amazing is that the Father sent his Son to be the Saviour of the world. It is better to trust in him than anyone else. He saves us from death. Do you thank him for that?

QUESTION, ANSWER AND MEMORY

91. What do we deserve for breaking the commandments?
God's anger and punishment. (Romans 6:23)
92. How can we escape from God's anger and punishment?
God, in his mercy, has provided the only way of escape through faith in the Lord Jesus Christ for those who repent. (Acts 20:21)

MEMORY VERSE 43
Let the little children come to Me, and do not forbid them; for of such is the kingdom of God (Mark 10:14 NKJV). Jesus told his disciples to allow the little children to come to him. They were not to turn them away. Jesus still wants little children to come to him.

THINGS TO DO

Make a list of countries around the world where the church is in need of prayer. Write down what these people need help with. Keep your list beside the radio or television so that when you hear about these countries in the news you can pray for the church there.

301. Glory, Honour and Power

(Revelation 4:11)

Worthy are you, our Lord and God,
to receive glory
and honour and power,
for you created all things,
and by your will,
they existed and were created.

At times, the world seems to be out of control. But if you could look into heaven, what would you see? Something too wonderful to describe: God sitting on a throne. Nothing exists unless he made it. Nothing happens unless he allows it. That is why all of heaven never stops worshipping him, and you must do the same.

302. The Church

(Isaiah 64:8-9)

LORD, you are our Father,
we are the clay,
and you are our potter;
we are all the work of your hand.
Be not so terribly angry, O LORD,
and remember not
iniquity forever.

Churches become weak when the LORD's people wander from his ways. Does that make you sad? Then cry to God for help. He made the church and it is his family. Ask him to forgive us because Jesus came from heaven to save his people.

303. My Heart is Sick

(Jeremiah 17:9, 14)

My heart is deceitful above all things
and desperately sick.
Heal me, O LORD, and I shall be healed;
save me and I shall be saved,
for you are the one I praise.

The LORD is a fountain of living water. He satisfies us and gives us endless life. So why do we turn away from him? It is because our hearts are sick. We think that we can succeed without God. Thankfully, he knows our crazy thoughts and is able to make us completely better.

304. God is Not Forgetful

(Psalm 25:7)

Do not remember the sins of my youth
or my transgressions;
remember me according to
your loving kindness,
for the sake of your goodness,
O LORD.

God is not forgetful. He is able to remember everything. That is bad news because we have sinned against God. It is also good news since he never forgets to be merciful. We know that because, by his blood, Jesus freed his people from their sins. That means you can ask him to forget your sins.

305. Christ Gave Himself

(Galatians 2:20)

Give me faith to believe
that the Son of God
loved me
and gave himself
for me.

What will make God accept you? Not the good things you do. Jesus alone can make you good enough for God. You must believe that he loved you and gave his life for you. There is no other way to please God.

306. God is a Spirit

(1 Chronicles 29:10; John 4:24)

O LORD,
the God of Israel,
our Father,
forever and ever,
you are spirit;
help me to worship you
in spirit and in truth.

Y ou cannot see God. He is spirit. So how can you worship him? Only with the help of his Spirit and as the Bible teaches you. That means you can only worship God through Jesus. You need his Holy Spirit to show you that Jesus is the truth.

307. We Need the Holy Spirit

(John 14:26)

Send your Holy Spirit
to teach me all things
and remind me of
everything Jesus said.

A fter Jesus was on earth, he asked his Father to send the Holy Spirit to his disciples. The Spirit came. He helped them to talk and write about what Jesus said and did. You still need to ask for the Spirit's help. Without him, you will never really understand what they wrote in the Bible.

308. Jesus' Cry on the Cross

(Psalm 22:1-2; Matthew 27:46)

My God, my God,
why have you forsaken me?
Why are you so far from saving me,
from the words of my groaning?
O my God, I cry by day,
but you do not answer,
and by night, but I find no rest.

Do you ever keep praying and nothing happens? Do you think God has forgotten you? Feeling like that can bring you to know Jesus better. When he was being crucified, he felt that God had left him. That is why you can be certain God always rescues those who trust in him.

QUESTION, ANSWER AND MEMORY

93. What is faith?
Faith in Jesus Christ is a gift from God, when we trust in him completely to save us from sin. (John 3:16)

94. What is repentance?
Repentance is a gift from God. We are made to be truly sorry for our sins. We turn from them to Jesus Christ. We live to please him. (Luke 18:13)

MEMORY VERSE 44
Repent therefore and be converted, that your sins may be blotted out (Acts 3:19 NKJV). To repent means to be truly sorry for our evil thoughts, words and actions. We want to stop sinning and please God.

309. Are You Wise?

(Proverbs 3:5)

LORD, help me to trust in you
with all my heart
and not to lean upon
my own understanding.

What do you think of yourself? Are you wise? If you think you are wise, then you are not. It is a mistake to imagine that you are clever enough to make your own plans. You will only be wise when you completely trust in the LORD and not at all in yourself.

310. Jesus Came to Save the Lost

(1 Peter 2:25; Psalm 119:176)

Shepherd and Guardian of my soul,
I have gone astray
like a lost sheep.
Seek your servant,
for I do not forget
your commandments.

Travelling somewhere for the first time, you might not notice if you get lost. But by the hundredth journey, you know when you make a mistake. The better you know God's commands, the sooner you will realise when you go wrong. The good news is that Jesus came to save the lost. He protects the lives of his people.

311. Be Content

(1 Timothy 1:1; 6:7-8)

God our Saviour,
I brought nothing into the world
and I can take nothing out of it.
If I have food and clothing,
make me content with that.

Those who want to get rich do not love Jesus. And when they get into the church, they quarrel and only help themselves. But if God is your Saviour, you understand that anything you gain from the world will be left behind when you die. So you should be happy with whatever he gives you and wherever he puts you.

312. Walk Humbly with God

(Micah 6:8)

LORD,
help me to do what you require:
to act justly, to love mercy,
and to walk humbly with you,
my God.

What does the LORD expect of you? You might think that going to church is what matters. But God hates it when you sing and pray if you do not want to do what is right every day. If you say you love him, he expects you to love others and to remember that he is your King.

313. Lord of lords

(Deuteronomy 10:17; Malachi 1:11)

God of gods and Lord of lords,
the great, the mighty,
and the awesome God,
from the rising sun
to where it sets,
let your name be great
among the nations.

All over the world, Jesus is worshipped as God. He is greater than all other gods. There is no one like him. He is powerful, merciful, and fair. You can pray that everyone would learn that he is Lord of lords. God promised that people in every place would worship him.

QUESTION, ANSWER AND MEMORY

95. How does God help us to experience his salvation?
By his Word, the Bible, the sacraments and prayer. (Acts 2:42. 2 Timothy 3:15)
96. How should we read the Word?
We should read the Bible carefully and believe all of it. (2 Timothy 3:16)

MEMORY VERSE 45
But the fruit of the Spirit is love, joy, peace, longsuffering, kindness, goodness, faithfulness, gentleness, self-control (Galatians 5:22-23 NKJV). If God the Holy Spirit is guiding you, faith will be shown in your life along with the other fruit of the Spirit.

314. Thank God

(Psalm 57:9-10)

I will give thanks to you, O Lord,
among the peoples;
I will sing praises to you
among the nations.
For your loving-kindness
reaches the heavens,
your faithfulness to the clouds.

The Lord will never love you in a small way. You cannot measure his constant kindness. It would be easier to take a ruler and work out the distance to the sun. The proper thing to do is to thank him. The whole world must know that no other god is like our God.

315. Want What God Wants

(1 John 5:14)

Give me this confidence in you,
that if I ask for anything
according to your will,
you will hear me.

God is a father who gives his children anything they ask for. It is not that you can make God do whatever you like. It is because if you are one of his children, you want what he wants. So when you pray, you love to ask for things that please him. You can be sure that he hears.

316. Keep God's Commands

(Proverbs 4:18)

Keep me on the path
of the righteous,
which like the light of dawn,
shines brighter and brighter
until the full day.

If you live to please God, then you listen to his words and keep his commands. They show you the way to go. Forget to follow his directions and you will get lost in the dark. But if you remember his teaching, you will grow wiser and stronger until you see God.

317. God's Good Work in You

(Philippians 1:10)

Work in me
so that I will be able
to choose what is best
and so be pure and blameless
in the day of Jesus Christ.

Is God doing his good work in you? Then you love to please him. Not to break his law is good, but that is the least you want to do. You long to give him everything because Jesus is coming soon. When he comes, will he see that you chose the best things for the best reasons?

318. King of kings

(Revelation 19:16; Psalm 45:3, 4)

King of kings and Lord of lords,
clothe yourself
with splendour and majesty.
Ride forth victoriously;
let your right hand display
awesome deeds.

Jesus is a warrior. But he is no ordinary soldier. He fights for truth and righteousness. Jesus never loses. His enemies looked strong when he was crucified, but Satan could not hold our Saviour. No one who fights against Jesus can succeed. One day everyone will realise that he is the great and powerful King.

319. Hear God's Voice

(Psalm 95:8, 11; Hebrews 3:4)

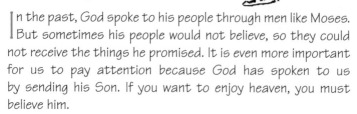

Let me hear your voice today.
Do not let me harden my heart
because I want to
enter your rest.

In the past, God spoke to his people through men like Moses. But sometimes his people would not believe, so they could not receive the things he promised. It is even more important for us to pay attention because God has spoken to us by sending his Son. If you want to enjoy heaven, you must believe him.

Let's Think About

THE PSALMS

NOTE FROM THE AUTHOR

The Book of Psalms is the longest book in the Bible. Psalms means 'praises' and God has given us this book to help us to praise him in different ways and at different times.

The Book of Psalms has many authors, but King David composed lots of them. Some Psalms are happy, others sad or complaining. No matter what mood we are in, there is always a Psalm to suit our need.

Jesus knew the Psalms well. He would have learned them as a boy. He quoted from them. He would sing them regularly.

Although the Psalms have different authors, themes and expressions, they have one thing in common – they are all centred on the one and only living God.

QUESTION, ANSWER AND MEMORY

97. What are the sacraments of the church?
The sacraments are Baptism and the Lord's Supper.
(Matthew 28:19-20)

MEMORY VERSE 46
Now faith is the substance of things hoped for, the evidence of things not seen (Hebrews 11:1 NKJV). Faith is a gift from God, when we trust him completely and believe what he tells us in his Word.

320. Our Great God

Great is the LORD, and greatly to be praised, and his greatness is unsearchable. (Psalm 145:3)

God is so great that we can never fully understand it. We can just praise him with all our hearts, and be glad that we have such a great God.

321. Our Steadfast God

Because your steadfast love is better than life, my lips will praise you. (Psalm 63:3)

When we think of the amazing love of God, we will want to praise him. His love is steadfast – it never stops. He loves us with an everlasting love.

322. Glorify God

My mouth is filled with your praise, and with your glory all the day. (Psalm 71:8)

We can use our mouths to speak about God and to sing praise to him. We can tell others how good he is and what he has done for us. It is so amazing that he sent his Son, the Lord Jesus, to save his people from their sins.

323. God is Good

Praise the LORD! For it is good to sing praises to our God; for it is pleasant, and a song of praise is fitting. (Psalm 147:1)

When we are happy, it is good to sing praise to the Lord. When we are sad, it is still good to sing praise to God. When we think of God's goodness, we don't feel so sad any more.

CONFIDENCE

324. God is Our Shepherd

The LORD is my shepherd; I shall not want. He makes me lie down in green pastures. He leads me beside still waters. (Psalm 23:1-2)

A good shepherd looks after his sheep, finding plenty grass for them to eat and water to drink. He keeps them safe from wild animals. Jesus is the Good Shepherd who not only feeds and protects his people, but laid down his life for them so that their sins would be forgiven and they would receive eternal life.

325. Our Help Comes from God

My help comes from the LORD, who made heaven and earth. (Psalm 121:2)

When we feel anxious or troubled, the best helper is the Lord God. He is always with us. He never goes to sleep. We can ask him to keep us from danger and temptation and sin.

326. God Gives Us Sleep

In peace I will both lie down and sleep; for you alone, O LORD, make me dwell in safety. (Psalm 4:8)

A good night's sleep is a great blessing from God. You can go to bed very tired and weary and wake up in the morning refreshed. Only God is able to keep us safe. Trust in him when you lie down to sleep.

327. The Lord is My Light

The Lord is my light and my salvation; whom shall I fear? The Lord is the stronghold of my life; of whom shall I be afraid? (Psalm 27:1)

Sometimes we can feel afraid in the dark. The darkness of sin can be frightening too. But God's light dispels the darkness. He promises salvation to all who trust in him.

SADNESS

328. Forgiver of Sin

Consider my affliction and my trouble, and forgive all my sins. (Psalm 25:18)

The big problem that we have is our sin. God hates it and has to punish it because he is holy. But Jesus took the punishment for the sins of his people. Because of his death, their sins are forgiven.

329. God Hears

When the righteous cry for help, the LORD hears and delivers them out of all their troubles. (Psalm 34:17)

When we are sad or in trouble, the best thing to do is to cry to God for help. God hears our prayers and is ready to help. Those who trust in the Lord Jesus are at last taken to heaven where there is no trouble or sadness.

QUESTION, ANSWER AND MEMORY

98. What is Baptism?
Baptism is the outward sign of washing with water, in the name of the Father, and of the Son and of the Holy Spirit, which tells us about the cleansing from sin by the blood of Jesus Christ and about belonging to God. (Acts 2:38-41)

MEMORY VERSE 47
In God I have put my trust; I will not be afraid. What can man do to me? (Psalm 56:11 NKJV). When we trust in God, we do not need to be afraid of what others will do to us or say about us.

330. God is Love

As for me, I am poor and needy, but the Lord takes thought for me. You are my help and my deliverer; do not delay, O my God! (Psalm 40:17)

There are 7 billion people in the world. How small and insignificant you are. But God knows you and thinks about you. God loves his people so much that he sent his Son to die on the cross to save them from their sin.

JOY

331. Sing to the Lord

Oh come, let us sing to the Lord; let us make a joyful noise to the rock of our salvation! (Psalm 95:1)

When we are happy we like to sing. When we remember how good God is to us, it should make us feel like singing. God is so good that he worked out a plan to save us from our sins through his Son, the Lord Jesus.

332. God's Day

This is the day that the LORD has made; let us rejoice and be glad in it. (Psalm 118:24)

God has made every day and we have good reason to rejoice every day. Some days, like your Birthday, are special days and we can be especially glad for God's blessings that day. The Lord's Day, or Sunday, is a special day each week when we can rejoice and worship God.

333. Be Glad

Make a joyful noise to the LORD, all the earth! Serve the LORD with gladness! Come into his presence with singing! (Psalm 100:1-2)

How can a young boy or girl serve the Lord? One way is by singing praise to him with gladness. This is pleasing to God.

COMFORT IN TROUBLE

334. God is So Loving

As a father shows compassion to his children, so the LORD shows compassion to those who fear him. (Psalm 103:13)

When a little child falls and hurts himself, he wants to go to his mother or father to be comforted. God is the most loving father who comforts his children when they are down.

335. God's Promises

This is my comfort in my affliction, that your promise gives me life. (Psalm 119:50)

No matter how big the problem is, God's promises are bigger. He has promised eternal life to all who trust in him. When we think of that, our problems seem much smaller.

QUESTION, ANSWER AND MEMORY

99. What is the Lord's Supper?
The Lord's Supper is the outward sign of eating bread and drinking wine which tells us about the death of the Lord Jesus Christ for his people. (1 Corinthians 11:23)
100. What do the bread and wine represent?
The body of Christ and the blood of Christ. (1 Corinthians 11:24-25)

336. Refuge and Safety

God is our refuge and strength, a very present help in trouble. (Psalm 46:1)

When a sailor is out on the stormy sea, he is longing to reach the refuge or safety of the harbour. God is like that safe place, rescuing us from the storms of life.

MEMORY VERSE 48
I have learned in whatever state I am, to be content (Philippians 4:11 NKJV). God provides all our needs. It is best not to be envious of what others have but to be content or happy with what God has given us. Paul had learned this.

337. God is My Strength

My flesh and my heart may fail, but God is the strength of my heart and my portion forever. (Psalm 73:26)

Even when we become old and sick and frail, God's strength will sustain us. He will never leave or forsake his people.

GOD'S NAME

338. God is Majestic

O LORD, our Lord, how majestic is your name in all the earth! You have set your glory above the heavens. (Psalm 8:1)

God is described as the King of kings – the most important king of all. He is worthy of all honour and glory. Everything about God is majestic and glorious.

339. Praise Him

From the rising of the sun to its setting, the name of the LORD is to be praised! (Psalm 113:3)

God is to be praised all day long — from our first waking thoughts in the morning until we drift off to sleep at night. We can pray to God at any time and in any place.

340. Worship Him

Ascribe to the LORD the glory due his name; bring an offering and come into his courts. (Psalm 96:8)

God wants us to worship him at all times. It is good to come to his house (the church) to worship with his people. What offering does he want? He wants our hearts of love and trust and obedience to his Word.

CREATION

341. The Heavens Declare

The heavens declare the glory of God, and the sky above proclaims his handiwork. (Psalm 19:1)

We only have to look at the sky to be reminded of God's power and greatness. The heavens are vast and high above the earth. God's ways are even vaster and so much higher than our ways, and his thoughts are higher than our thoughts.

342. The Earth is the Lord's

The earth is the LORD's and the fullness thereof, the world and those who dwell therein, for he has founded it upon the seas and established it upon the rivers. (Psalm 24:1-2)

God made the whole world and everything in it. Everything belongs to him and is under his loving control. God cares for everything that he has made. Without him we can do nothing.

343. In The Beginning

By the word of the LORD the heavens were made, and by the breath of his mouth all their host. (Psalm 33:6)

In the beginning, God created the heavens and the earth. God made all things from nothing by the word of his power – the light, the heavens, the land, the trees, the stars and us too.

QUESTION, ANSWER AND MEMORY

101. Why did Jesus Christ command this sacrament to be kept by those who trust in him?
So that his suffering and death would be remembered and proclaimed till the end of the world. (1 Corinthians 11:26)

MEMORY VERSE 49
And now abide faith, hope, love, these three; but the greatest of these is love (1 Corinthians 13:13 NKJV). Faith is a wonderful gift of God and so is hope. But the gift which will last throughout eternity is LOVE.

MISSION

344. Every Country

May his name endure forever, his fame continue as long as the sun! May people be blessed in him, all nations call him blessed. (Psalm 72:17)

God so loved the world that he sent his Son, so that all who trust in him will not perish, but have everlasting life. That love extends to every country of the world. Our prayer will be that God will draw many people to trust and love him.

345. Preach the Gospel

May God be gracious to us and bless us and make his face to shine upon us, that your way may be known on earth, your saving power among all nations. (Psalm 67:1-2)

Everybody needs to know about the Lord Jesus Christ. He told his disciples, just before he ascended into heaven, to preach the gospel right to the ends of the earth. Jesus' followers today are still doing that. Missionaries are working all over the world to pass on the good news about Jesus.

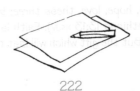

346. Pray for Christians

He has remembered his steadfast love and faithfulness to the house of Israel. All the ends of the earth have seen the salvation of our God. (Psalm 98:3)

There are Christians all over the world. Jesus is building his church in many different countries. We can pray for Christians in other lands and support them in practical ways.

CHILDREN

347. Teach Children

He (God) established a testimony in Jacob and appointed a law in Israel, which he commanded our fathers to teach to their children, that the next generation might know them ... (Psalm 78:5-6)

God wants fathers to teach their children about himself and his Word. The children then have to teach their children and on down through the generations. It is important that this chain is not broken.

223

348. How Wisdom Begins

Come, O children, listen to me; I
will teach you the fear of the LORD.
(Psalm 34:11)

Respect for God the Lord is
the beginning of wisdom. We
learn about God in his Word, the
Bible. Instruction is given about
what we are to believe about God.
We learn of his plan of salvation
through the Lord Jesus Christ.
We are told how to behave in a
way that is pleasing to God. That
teaching is worth listening to.

349. The Kingdom of Heaven

Out of the mouth of babies and infants, you have established
strength because of your foes, to still the enemy and the avenger.
(Psalm 8:2)

Even young children can be used by God to praise him, so
that his enemies are silenced. God is able to use the
weak things of the world to shame the mighty. Jesus loved
the children. He said that the kingdom of heaven belonged
to them.

MERCY

350. God Shows Mercy

Have mercy on me, O God, according to your steadfast love; according to your abundant mercy blot out my transgressions. (Psalm 51:1)

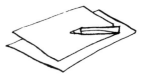

Our sin deserves God's punishment. But God shows mercy to those who confess and forsake their sin and who trust in the Lord Jesus Christ who died to save sinners.

QUESTION, ANSWER AND MEMORY

102. What is prayer?
Prayer is asking God for things that are agreeable to him, confessing our sins to him and thanking him for all his mercies. (Philippians 4:6)
103. In whose name should we pray?
In the name of Jesus Christ. (John 16:23)

MEMORY VERSE 50
While the earth remains, seedtime and harvest, cold and heat, summer and winter, day and night, shall not cease (Genesis 8:22). The seasons of the year, the weather, the darkness of the night and the light of the day are all under the control of God.

351. A Very Short Prayer

O Lord, hear my voice! Let your ears be attentive to the voice of my pleas for mercy! (Psalm 130:2)

Jesus told us about a man who prayed a very short prayer, 'God be merciful to me a sinner' (Luke 18:13). We can have that prayer too.

352. Worshipping Forever

Surely goodness and mercy shall follow me all the days of my life, and I shall dwell in the house of the LORD forever. (Psalm 23:6)

God's goodness and mercy will never fail us. Those who know this, will love to be in God's house worshipping him. They will love to be in heaven with the Lord worshipping him forever.

GUIDANCE

353. God's Plan of Salvation

Lead me in your truth and teach me, for you are the God of my salvation; for you I wait all the day long. (Psalm 25:5)

God teaches us many things in his Word, but the main thing is his plan of salvation. The Lord Jesus Christ died to save sinners. The whole Bible is pointing to that wonderful event.

354. God Sees

I will instruct you and teach you in the way you should go; I will counsel you with my eye upon you. (Psalm 32:8)

God sees and knows everything we do. His watchful eye is always on us, correcting us when we go wrong and teaching us what is good and true and helpful.

355. Light and Truth

Send out your light and your truth; let them lead me; let them bring me to your holy hill and to your dwelling! (Psalm 43:3)

God's Word is the light to guide us and every word is true. Jesus Christ told us that he is 'the Light of the World'. Jesus is the best friend and the best guide for life.

356. God's Guidelines

Lead me in the path of your commandments, for I delight in it. (Psalm 119:35)

God has given us clear guidelines in his Word, the Ten Commandments. These are not meant to be a burden to us, but with God's help, they will be a blessing and delight to us.

OUR LOVE FOR GOD

357. When We Pray

I love the LORD, because he has heard my voice and my pleas for mercy. (Psalm 116:1)

Our love for God is shown when we pray to him. When he hears our cries for mercy and answers them (and he loves to do that), then we will love him even more.

QUESTION, ANSWER AND MEMORY

104. What has God given us to teach us to pray?
The whole Bible teaches us about prayer but Jesus especially teaches us about it in the Lord's Prayer. (Matthew 6:9-13)
105. What is the Lord's Prayer?
The Lord's Prayer is:-
Our Father in heaven,
Hallowed be your name.
Your kingdom come.
Your will be done on earth as it is in heaven.
Give us today our daily bread.
Forgive us our debts as we also have forgiven our debtors.
And lead us not into temptation but deliver us from evil.
For yours is the kingdom and the power and the glory forever.
Amen. (Matthew 6:9-13)

MEMORY VERSE 51
Casting all your care upon Him; for He cares for you (1 Peter 5:7)
We should tell all our problems to God and ask him to help us. He loves and cares for us more than anyone else ever can.

358. Listen and Love

Oh, how I love your law! It is my meditation all the day. (Psalm 119:97)

If we love God, we will love to hear from him and to think about what he says to us in his Word, the Bible. We love him because he first loved us.

359. Depend on The Rock

I love you, O LORD, my strength. The LORD is my rock and my fortress and my deliverer, my God, my rock, in whom I take refuge, my shield, and the horn of my salvation, my stronghold. (Psalm 18:1-2)

When we think about our strong dependable God, who never changes, our hearts are drawn to him in love. We can be totally confident in his care and keeping.

GOD'S LOVE FOR US

360. God Cares For Us

Let your steadfast love, O LORD, be upon us, even as we hope in you. (Psalm 33:22)

To hope in God is to be confident and trust in his promises. God's many promises should assure us of his love and care for us.

361. God's Love Never Fails

Show us your steadfast love, O LORD, and grant us your salvation. (Psalm 85:7)

God's love is steadfast. It never fails. It never grows cold. His love is most evident when he sent the Lord Jesus Christ to this world to live and die and rise again from the dead. Salvation is given to us through this finished work of the Lord Jesus.

362. God is Gracious

The LORD is merciful and gracious, slow to anger and abounding in steadfast love. (Psalm 103:8)

Our sins deserve immediate punishment, but God is merciful and gracious to us. His unfailing love to sinners means that his anger which we deserve was turned on Jesus Christ, God the Son. What a wonderful plan of salvation.

BLESSING

363. Love God's Word

Blessed is the man who walks not in the counsel of the wicked, nor stands in the way of sinners, nor sits in the seat of scoffers, but his delight is in the law of the LORD, and on his law he meditates day and night. (Psalm 1:1-2)

The company a person keeps has a big effect on his life. Wicked people who mock God and his Word, should be avoided. God's blessing or favour is with the person who loves God's Word and lives by it every day.

364. Forgiveness of Sin

Blessed is the one whose transgression is forgiven, whose sin is covered. (Psalm 32:1)

A great blessing from God is forgiveness of sin. This forgiveness comes through the grace of God. Our sins are blotted out through the death and resurrection of Jesus Christ.

~~~~~~~~~~~~~~~~~~~~

QUESTION, ANSWER AND MEMORY

106 Did Christ stay in the grave after he died?
No. He rose from the dead on the third day. (Matthew 28:6)
107. Where is Christ now?
He is in heaven, sitting at the right hand of God the Father, praying always for his people. (Mark 16:19)
108. Will he come to the world again?
Yes. At the end of time, Christ will come to judge the world. (Matthew 25:31-32)

MEMORY VERSE 52
And we know that all things work together for good to those who love God, to those who are the called according to his purpose (Romans 8:28 NKJV). The person who is called to follow God, and loves him, can be confident that all the experiences will have some good purpose.

365. Do Not Worry

May the LORD give strength to his people! May the LORD bless his people with peace! (Psalm 29:11)

The Lord has told us not to be anxious about anything, but to commit everything to him in prayer. Then the peace of God will guard our hearts and minds in Christ Jesus.

INSTRUCTIONS

366. Be Careful of Your Tongue

Keep your tongue from evil and your lips from speaking deceit. Turn away from evil and do good, seek peace and pursue it. (Psalm 34:13-14)

Our tongue can get us into a lot of trouble – a hasty remark, a lie, a cruel reply. These little words can be the start of a big problem. We should use our tongue to speak good, kind and truthful words.

367. Peace and Harmony

Behold, how good and pleasant it is when brothers dwell in unity. (Psalm 133:1)

Parents love to see their children playing happily and peaceably together. God loves to see his children living in peace and harmony. When Christians quarrel and disagree, it is grieving to the Lord.

368. Your Reward

Delight yourself in the LORD, and he will give you the desires of your heart. (Psalm 37:4)

If we delight in the Lord, our heart's desire will be him. He will be our reward. We could not wish for anything better.

369. God is Just

Remember not the sins of my youth or my transgressions: according to your steadfast love remember me, for the sake of your goodness, O LORD! (Psalm 25:7)

If we confess our sins, God is faithful and just to forgive us our sins and to cleanse us from all unrighteousness. He does not hold these sins against us, but casts them into the depths of the sea (Micah 7:19).

370. Trust in Him

For you, O LORD, are my hope, my trust LORD, from my youth. (Psalm 71:5)

From the day of our birth, all through life, the Lord is in control of all that happens. He wants us to trust in him when we are young. You are never too young to serve the Lord.

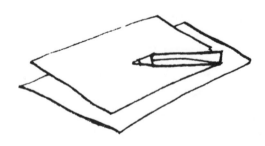

371. Guard Against Sin

How can a young man keep his way pure? By guarding it according to your word. (Psalm 119:9)

Sin can easily slip into our minds and our words and actions. God tells us to be on guard against sin by reading and obeying his Word. This is important for young and old.

~~~~~~~~~~

QUESTION, ANSWER AND MEMORY

109. What happens when a person dies?
The body decays but the soul lives on and goes either to heaven or to hell. (1 Thessalonians 4:14)
110. Will the bodies of the dead be raised again?
Yes. When Christ returns, the bodies of the dead will be raised and joined to their souls forever. (1 Corinthians 15:43)
111. Where does God send the wicked?
To hell. (Matthew 25:41)

MEMORY VERSE 53
I love those who love me; and those who seek me diligently will find me (Proverbs 8:17 NKJV). God's love is pure and true and everlasting. We can only love him in a weak and imperfect way. But he understands us. God wants us to love and serve him when we are young.

QUESTION, ANSWER AND MEMORY

112. What is hell?
A terrible place of torment and punishment. (Luke 16:28)
113. Where does the godly person go at death?
To heaven. (Matthew 25:34)
114. What is heaven?
A glorious joyful place where Christ is. (Revelation 21:4)

MEMORY VERSE 54
The joy of the LORD is your strength (Nehemiah 8:10 NKJV). Even when things are difficult, God gives his people a sense of peace and joy. This gives them the strength to go on and follow and trust him.

Scripture Index
OLD TESTAMENT

RUTH:

20

1 AND 2 SAMUEL:

21, 155

1 AND 2 KINGS:

128

1 AND 2 CHRONICLES:

137, 198

NEHEMIAH:

86, 191, 238

JOB:

19, 22, 55, 75, 167

PSALMS:

18, 22, 23, 24, 27, 43, 49, 52, 56, 59, 61-65, 67, 69, 70, 79, 83, 84, 87, 97, 105, 117, 131-134, 142, 147, 148, 150, 152, 158, 159, 163, 164, 168, 169, 170, 171, 176, 177, 178, 180, 181, 182, 184, 189, 190, 193, 194, 197, 199, 200, 203, 205, 209-228, 230-237

PROVERBS:

12, 15, 17, 20, 27, 28, 66, 132, 133, 148, 155, 157, 160, 186, 200, 204, 237

NEW TESTAMENT

MATTHEW:

11, 14, 18, 21, 34, 37, 53, 54, 61, 79, 85, 89, 91, 95, 96, 97, 101, 102, 104, 106, 107, 111, 116, 119, 124, 132, 133, 144, 147, 149, 161, 169, 193, 199, 208, 229, 233, 237, 238

MARK:

30, 46, 48, 49, 83, 88, 99, 100, 108, 109, 110, 116, 118, 119, 135, 137, 156, 192, 194, 233

LUKE:

13, 31, 36, 65, 91, 95, 98, 99, 102, 103, 104, 107, 108, 113, 118, 120, 133, 154, 155, 165, 166, 174, 178, 179, 199, 238

JOHN:

12, 17, 19, 38, 40-42, 54, 57, 61, 65, 69, 80, 82, 84, 87, 91, 94, 102, 105, 106, 108, 110, 112, 114, 115, 117, 121, 124, 125, 134, 136, 138, 140, 141, 142, 144, 155, 160, 162, 185, 198, 199, 225

ACTS:

48, 74, 75, 76, 81, 85, 87, 88, 89, 91, 92, 117, 121, 122, 123, 131, 139, 145, 155, 156, 176, 194, 199, 202, 213

ROMANS:

11, 24, 26, 31, 35, 41, 55, 65, 68, 75, 79, 81, 86, 87, 101, 113, 117, 121, 139, 180, 186, 190, 194, 233

1 AND 2 CORINTHIANS:

13, 14, 19, 32, 36, 42, 66, 74, 77, 78, 82, 88, 125, 150, 179, 182, 187, 216, 221, 237

GALATIANS:

14, 15, 16, 18, 20, 22, 25, 90, 197, 202

EPHESIANS:

11, 13, 17, 26, 30, 32, 34, 44, 60, 77, 78, 79, 87, 125, 166, 192

PHILIPPIANS:

12, 16, 22, 23, 49, 130, 150, 165, 169, 191, 192, 204, 217, 225

COLOSSIANS:

15, 19, 33, 76, 121, 165

1 THESSALONIANS:

26, 46, 82, 156, 237

1 AND 2 TIMOTHY:

12, 14, 17, 23, 28, 43, 44, 57, 58, 68, 85, 86, 90, 122, 154, 159, 162, 174, 176, 184, 201, 202

HEBREWS:

12, 24, 41, 43, 45, 76, 83, 84, 97, 101, 105, 117, 122, 124, 128, 129, 149, 151, 158, 161, 169, 176, 190, 205, 208

JAMES:

10, 18, 25, 145, 146, 177, 191

1 AND 2 PETER:

26, 47, 78, 129, 136, 168, 185, 189, 190, 200, 229

1 JOHN:

20, 33, 37, 41, 63, 67, 77, 78, 82, 140, 146, 184, 203

REVELATION:

17, 45, 74, 156, 160, 176, 195, 205, 238

Topical Index

Each of these words would make a good study for you and your family. These numbers are not page numbers but the numbers of each daily reading. The Memory Verses and Questions and Answers are also indexed.

GOD THE FATHER
30, 67, 68, 123, 140, 160, 166, 181, 202, 225, 227 285, 293

GOD THE SON
1, 15, 34, 36, 67, 69, 84, 93, 110, 123, 130, 131, 142, 146, 160, 156-161, 173, 179, 227, 239, 248, 305
MEMORY VERSE: 17, 25

GRACE
1, 4, 15, 33, 54, 81, 84, 111, 113, 234, 251, 262, 279, 364
MEMORY VERSE: 27, 34

HEAVEN
15, 16, 39, 45, 52, 56, 68, 74, 76, 77, 103, 110, 112, 113, 148, 158, 160, 165, 177, 178, 179, 182, 212, 216, 218, 277, 279, 295, 295, 302, 319, 329, 349, 352
Q&A: 42, 107, 105, 109, 113, 114
MEMORY VERSE: 17, 25, 28

HOLY SPIRIT
9, 41, 58, 64, 67, 70, 101, 123, 127, 132, 140, 202, 238, 245, 246, 255, 306, 307
Q&A: 6, 18, 47, 55, 98
MEMORY VERSE: 17, 45

JOY
3, 16, 36, 45, 57, 109, 127, 167, 177, 254, 256, 277, 287, 331-333
Q&A: 114
MEMORY VERSE: 31, 45, 54

LIFE

1, 16, 20, 23, 26, 28, 36, 37, 39, 48, 50, 52, 55, 64, 72, 76, 79, 80, 87, 97, 102, 109, 119, 127, 128, 130, 143, 147, 159, 165, 168, 194, 199, 201, 209, 216, 233, 235, 250, 259, 271, 287, 299, 303, 305, 327, 336, 370

Q&A: 43, 80

MEMORY VERSE: 11, 12, 13, 21, 25, 45

LOVE

1, 8, 17, 18, 24, 29, 41, 42, 43, 51, 53, 61, 65, 69, 70, 71, 78, 82, 84, 85, 89, 90, 93, 103, 105, 109, 110, 112, 113, 114, 125, 127, 148, 151, 154, 159, 164, 167, 172, 178, 192, 195, 209, 214, 237, 254, 256, 260, 274, 278, 290, 296, 305, 312, 314, 321, 330, 344, 346, 349, 350, 357-359, 360-362, 363, 369

Q&A: 63-65, 69, 78

MEMORY VERSE: 6, 17, 26, 34, 41, 45, 49, 51, 52, 53

PEACE

23, 25, 35, 38, 56, 109, 111, 114, 127, 167, 181, 193, 230, 232, 256, 287, 326, 365, 366, 367

MEMORY VERSE: 9, 45, 54

SALVATION

16, 33, 36, 41, 42, 88, 110, 137, 156, 166, 171, 178, 180, 197, 208, 237, 251, 266, 327, 331, 348, 353, 361, 362

Q&A: 95

MEMORY VERSE: 27, 28, 31, 39

Questions and Answers

Throughout the book there are 114 different questions and answers. Try and memorize as many as you can. Photocopy the following pages and every time you memorize a Q&A tick one of the books.

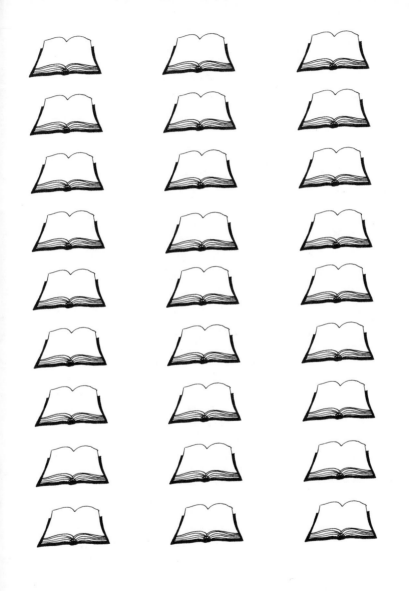

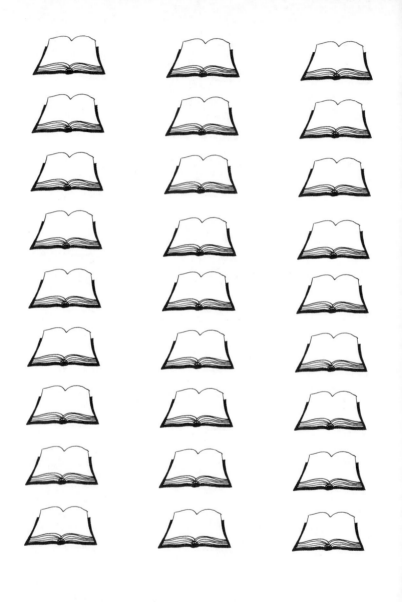

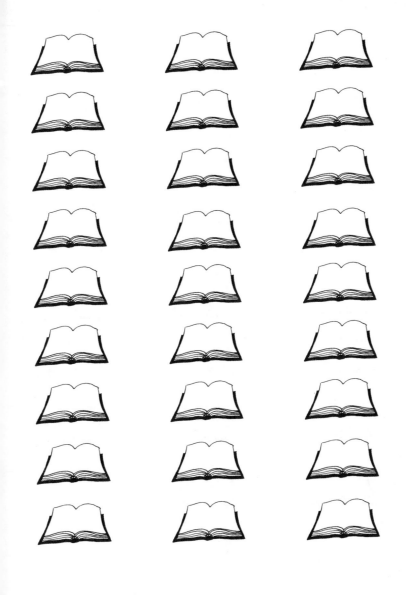

Endorsements for

My First Book of Questions and Answers

Truth, clarity and simplicity are the great virtues of this God-exalting catechism for children. It was a great pleasure to watch our daughter learn these answers. As usual, teaching a child great truths about God enriched our own thinking and intensified our own worship.

JOHN AND NOEL PIPER

Giving our children basic instruction in the faith is one of the primary responsibilities we have as Christian parents. Using this Children's Catechism is an ideal way of doing this. Here are the essential questions with the single-sentence, easily remembered answers. This is God-centred, Christ-honouring, life-transforming, character-building teaching – a long term investment in a few pages.

SINCLAIR B. FERGUSON

The doctrines of Scripture in contemporary language that is easy to memorize. This book is an effective, foundational tool for godly parents to use in catechizing their children.

JOEL BEEKE

I heartily recommend this children's catechism.

R.C. SPROUL

As Evangelicals, we have analysed the harmful cultural influences on our children but have been less effective in offering positive solutions to the problem. It is a joy, therefore, to recommend very highly Carine Mackenzie's new Catechism for children.

Here is something that Christian parents, grandparents and friends can do for the character development and wholesome spiritual growth of the young generation: teach them this catechism!

It is biblically sound throughout; a fine and clear summation of the structure of Reformed Theology. It is both comprehensive and comprehensible. Written in very plain and current English, it wastes no words and keeps to the point at issue in each question, and is organized so that theological concepts follow each other in proper order, much like its model, the Westminster Shorter Catechism.

It presents profound truth as simply as possible. As a father of five, I deem it to be happily accessible to children. It conveys a spirit of uplifting devotion.

This catechism could make a great difference in the lives of those who learn it. My prayer is that it may be very widely read.

DOUGLAS F. KELLY

RTS CHARLOTTE

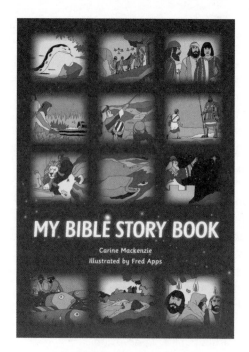

My Bible Story Book
by Carine Mackenzie

The stories in the Bible are adventures that happened to real men and women, boys and girls just like you, who lived during exciting times. They faced up to problems and danger with God's help. Perhaps they sometimes felt like giving up – but with God's strength they struggled on. Read about these amazing people in the Bible and begin your own adventure with God.

ISBN: 978-1-84550-129-7

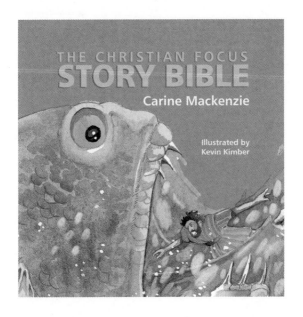

Christian Focus Story Bible
Carine Mackenzie

The Word of God is full of adventure, excitement and surprises. Look out for spies on a roof in Jericho and watch out for a Fiery Furnace in Babylon. There's a young boy who has killed a giant, and a little girl who has helped a brave soldier. There are lions, doves and a great big fish. One man and his family have to fit lots and lots of animals into a boat — but they have to make the boat first. The Bible is just full of wonderful stories like these.

ISBN: 978-1-84550-494-6

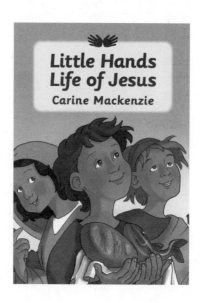

Little Hands Life of Jesus
by Carine Mackenzie

The life of Jesus is a story that will never end. His story is an adventure that you can join. It's a mystery that you can solve and it's a love story that's about you, God and his great, loving, wonderful heart; a heart that beats with a never-ending love for his people. Starting with the 'Important Announcement' and ending with Jesus' ascension this bible storybook retells the familiar stories in an engaging way that will have readers & their young listeners enthralled.

ISBN: 978-1-84550-339-0

Following God
by Carine Mackenzie

If you were standing underneath a plum tree you wouldn't expect to see bananas hanging there. If you reached up into the leaves of an apple tree you wouldn't pull down a coconut on top of your head. That just wouldn't happen. You know what sort of tree it is by its fruit and the Bible says that you know if someone is a Christian or not by the fruit of their lives. What sort of fruit is that?... well there is one fruit that is produced in a Christian and that is the Fruit of the Spirit. Find out about the different parts of this fruit by reading this book ... and by reading Galatians Chapter 5 from the Bible.

ISBN: 978-1-84550-750-3

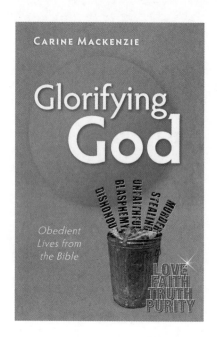

Glorifying God
by Carine Mackenzie

Find out about the ten commandments, God's rules
for our lives and about the only One who kept them as
they were meant to be kept – Jesus Christ, God's Son.
He is the answer to the problem of sin, and to our need
to get the better of it.

ISBN: 978-1-78191-124-2

Trusting God
by Carine Mackenzie

Do you know what your name means? Each year a list is compiled of the popular names given to babies born in that year. The list changes slightly year on year. God has many names that are truly unique. Carine has taken seven of God's names to explain them for children aged 7-11 years. Using a Bible story she shows them how these names of God are still relevant to us today. Your children will be fascinated by these new words.

ISBN: 978-1-84550-271-3

CHRISTIAN FOCUS PUBLICATIONS

Christian Focus | Christian Heritage | CF4K | Mentor

Christian Focus Publications publishes books for adults and children under its four main imprints: Christian Focus, CF4K, Mentor and Christian Heritage. Our books reflect our conviction that God's Word is reliable and Jesus is the way to know him, and live for ever with him.

Our children's publication list includes a Sunday School curriculum that covers pre-school to early teens, and puzzle and activity books. We also publish personal and family devotional titles, biographies and inspirational stories that children will love.

If you are looking for quality Bible teaching for children then we have an excellent range of Bible stories and age-specific theological books.

From pre-school board books to teenage apologetics, we have it covered!

Find us at our web page:
www.christianfocus.com

CF4·K
Because you're never
too young to know Jesus